Depressive Illness – The Curse of the Strong

Dr Tim Cantopher studied at University College, London and University College Hospital. He trained as a psychiatrist at St James' Hospital, Portsmouth and St George's Hospital Medical School. He has been a member of the Royal College of Psychiatrists since 1983 and was elected fellow of the college in 1999. He is now a consultant psychiatrist working with the Priory Group of Hospitals. This is Dr Cantopher's second book and he has published a number of research projects across psychiatry. Dr Cantopher is married wit

Overcoming Common Problems Series

Selected titles

A full list of titles is available from Sheldon Press,
36 Causton Street, London SW1P 4ST and on our website at
www.sheldonpress.co.uk

101 Questions to Ask Your Doctor
Dr Tom Smith

Birth Over 35
Sheila Kitzinger

Bulimia, Binge-eating and their Treatment
Professor J. Hubert Lacey, Dr Bryony Bamford
and Amy Brown

Coeliac Disease: What you need to know
Alex Gazzola

Coping Successfully with Shyness
Margaret Oakes, Professor Robert Bor
and Dr Carina Eriksen

Coping with Anaemia
Dr Tom Smith

Coping with Asthma in Adults
Mark Greener

Coping with Bronchitis and Emphysema
Dr Tom Smith

Coping with Drug Problems in the Family
Lucy Jolin

Coping with Dyspraxia
Jill Eckersley

Coping with Early-onset Dementia
Jill Eckersley

Coping with Envy
Dr Windy Dryden

Coping with Gout
Christine Craggs-Hinton

**Coping with Manipulation: When others
blame you for their feelings**
Dr Windy Dryden

**Coping with Obsessive Compulsive
Disorder**
Professor Kevin Gournay, Rachel Piper
and Professor Paul Rogers

Coping with Stomach Ulcers
Dr Tom Smith

Depressive Illness: The curse of the strong
Dr Tim Cantopher

**Divorce and Separation: A legal guide
for all couples**
Dr Mary Welstead

Dying for a Drink
Dr Tim Cantopher

**Epilepsy: Complementary and alternative
treatments**
Dr Sallie Baxendale

The Heart Attack Survival Guide
Mark Greener

High-risk Body Size: Take control of your weight
Dr Funké Baffour

How to Beat Worry and Stress
Dr David Delvin

How to Develop Inner Strength
Dr Windy Dryden

**Let's Stay Together: A guide to lasting
relationships**
Jane Butterworth

Living with IBS
Nuno Ferreira and David T. Gillanders

**Living with a Problem Drinker:
Your survival guide**
Rolande Anderson

Living with Tinnitus and Hyperacusis
Dr Laurence McKenna, Dr David Baguley
and Dr Don McFerran

Losing a Parent
Fiona Marshall

Making Sense of Trauma: How to tell your story
Dr Nigel C. Hunt and Dr Sue McHale

Motor Neurone Disease: A family affair
Dr David Oliver

Natural Treatments for Arthritis
Christine Craggs-Hinton

**Overcoming Gambling: A guide for problem
and compulsive gamblers**
Philip Mawer

Overcoming Loneliness
Alice Muir

**The Pain Management Handbook:
Your personal guide**
Neville Shone

Reducing Your Risk of Dementia
Dr Tom Smith

**Therapy for Beginners: How to get the best
out of counselling**
Professor Robert Bor, Sheila Gill and Anne Stokes

**Transforming Eight Deadly Emotions
into Healthy Ones**
Dr Windy Dryden

Treating Arthritis: The drug-free way
Margaret Hills and Christine Horner

Treating Arthritis: The supplements guide
Julia Davies

Overcoming Common Problems

Depressive Illness
The Curse of the Strong

Third edition

Dr Tim Cantopher

To the patients and staff who teach me

First published in Great Britain in 2003

Sheldon Press
36 Causton Street
London SW1P 4ST

Second edition published 2006
Third edition published 2012

British Library Cataloguing-in-Publication Data
A catalogue for this book is available from the British Library

ISBN 978-1-84709-235-9
eBook ISBN 978-1-84709-236-6

Typeset by Fakenham Prepress Solutions, Fakenham, Norfolk NR21 8NN
Printed and bound in Great Britain by
Ashford Colour Press

Subsequently digitally printed in Great Britain

Produced on paper from sustainable forests

Contents

Acknowledgements

I am indebted to the following friends and colleagues, who provided me with their time, wisdom and knowledge, thus allowing me to avoid demonstrating embarrassing areas of ignorance and to revise my most poorly judged prose:

Dr Paul Bailey
Mrs Natalie McMillan
Ms Annie Cygler
Mr Keith Mantle
Mr Rik Mullender
Ms Charlotte Cantopher

Thanks are also due to David Johnson and Sophie Dean for their excellent cartoons and to the Book Guild for allowing those which originally appeared in my first book *Dying for a Drink* to be reproduced here.

Introduction

'Oh, no! It's Monday morning. I don't want to get up. It's too early, the week is too long, I've got too much work to do and I need a holiday. I feel so depressed!'

Every Monday starts this way and I refuse to rise until I am running late, but after a while I drag myself grumpily out of bed and start my week.

I have never been good at Mondays and it takes a while for my mood to pick up through the day. It isn't that I don't like my job; I do, very much. It is just that I like rest and recreation even more and on a Monday morning the next opportunity for these pleasures seems an awfully long way away.

Everyone has suffered spells of low mood of this type at some time or other and some people think that this means everyone has suffered from depression. It doesn't, or at least, not *clinical depression* or *depressive illness*. The truth is that clinical depression is a horrible illness of which most of us, thank goodness, have not the faintest inkling. This is one of the many trials sufferers from the illness have to face: people looking at them knowingly and saying,

'Oh, yes, I've often had that. I find the best thing is just to pull myself together and get busy.'

No you haven't, so stop making things worse with your ill-informed advice. If you really want to help, try to understand that the sufferer of this illness is going through torment of a pretty awful kind. Among the descriptions of the experience of depressive illness that have impressed me are: 'It's like falling down a well with no bottom; the blackness surrounds you and the tiny circle of light gets ever smaller till it disappears', and 'It is being trapped in hell, with no comfort, no salvation and no hope.' Some Monday morning! To have the enormity of this experience understood may at least reduce the loneliness. That will mean a lot.

Part of the problem is in the name. Depression sounds like how I feel on a Monday morning, but in reality it isn't even close. The one is a relatively mild and transient disturbance of emotion, the other a serious illness causing immense suffering. When I'm in my more expansive moods, I would like to call it 'Cantopher's disease', as that sounds like a really serious condition, but if I did I think my colleagues would believe that I had finally gone over the edge into delusions of grandeur. The point, though, is a crucial one; the most important key to recovering from this illness is understanding that it is one.

There are many pieces of unhelpful advice to which sufferers of depressive illness are prone to be exposed. The commonest and possibly the worst is: 'Pull yourself together.' If I had a dollar for every time a patient of mine has had this injunction thrown at, I'd be Bill Gates. And it's so pointless. If the sufferer could have pulled himself together he would have done so ages ago. As you will read later, he is not the type to shirk challenges. In any case, what was the object of this stunning gem of advice? Do you really think he is going to put his hand to his brow and gasp: 'Gosh, thank you so much, I hadn't thought of that. Thank goodness you told me; I'll just go off and sort myself out and then everything will be fine'? I think not.

Beware, your advice can hurt and can potentially do serious harm. Better not to give any direction at all if you aren't sure. Understanding, patience and sympathy are in any case much more valuable commodities than even well-informed advice.

It is ironic that it is often the most loving friends and family who give the worst advice. They mean well and are calling from their own experience in their exhortations. 'Come on, get yourself going, get more interests, make more friends, get out more, let me show you how to have a good time.'

If you take this advice, good common sense though it seems to be, you will get much worse. But of course, it isn't just others who cause problems with their ignorance of this illness, it is also the sufferers themselves. I frequently find patients treating themselves with a harshness of a level they would never consider inflicting on anyone else. The guilt and self-loathing is in part a symptom of the illness, but in part it is also a cause of it. So stop condemning yourself for having the illness and don't make statements about yourself that you wouldn't make about another person. Would you say about a friend who was suffering from a severe and debilitating illness: 'Look at her, she is so weak and lazy, it's pathetic. She should get a grip and stop being so feeble!' I don't think so. Well, if unfair condemnation of the afflicted isn't right about others, it is wrong for you too. So stop it and show yourself some understanding. A start will be finding out about what your illness really is.

The rest of us, then, happily don't know how it feels to suffer from clinical depression. But what is this illness, who gets it, why does it happen and what can be done? This book will seek to answer these questions, though I must stress that I am writing only about one form of depression: that is, stress-induced depressive illness. Some of what I say doesn't apply to manic depressive illness (or bipolar affective disorder), to depression relating to bereavement, to depression complicating other illnesses, postnatal depression, Seasonal Affective Disorder (SAD), or to depression as part of long-term personality problems. These are separate afflictions with their own body of excellent literature and I will deal with them only in passing. Having said this, depression from whichever source responds well to many of the strategies outlined here, so if you suffer from one of these conditions, please do read on.

You won't find here a comprehensive account of all the different ways that depressive illness has been viewed and explained; I have included only theories and treatments that I think make sense. What you will find is the sum of what my patients have taught me and, as they're an impressive bunch of people, I think we can learn from their wisdom, experiences and mistakes. This doesn't mean they are all super-intelligent high-fliers; far from it. Most of the people who I have treated with this condition have earned my admiration and respect, but this has been for a range of different achievements. A mother who tries her best for her five children on income support, or a refugee coping with the hostility of his neighbours, while busting a gut for his family, are as much at risk of this illness as the president of Oxfam. What they have in common is what this book is about, and I love them for it.

One more thing. If you are in the middle of a severe depressive illness, you won't be able to concentrate for long. Don't try to read more than a page or two at a time. You will forget a lot, so re-read what you need to. Concentrate on **Chapters 1 and 5** for now. You can read the rest when you're a bit better and can concentrate for longer. Before we start, though, take heart. *People recover from depressive illness and can stay well if they make the right choices.*

1

What is depressive illness?

There are a lot of different ways of looking at depressive illness. I will touch on some of these in Chapter 3, but for now I want to focus on what I believe to be the most important aspect of it, which is this: depressive illness is not a psychological or emotional state and is not a mental illness. It is not a form of madness.

It is a physical illness.

This is not a metaphor; it is a fact. Clinical depression is every bit as physical a condition as pneumonia, or a broken leg. If I were to perform a lumbar puncture on my patients (which, new patients of mine will be pleased to hear, I don't) I would be able to demonstrate in the chemical analysis of the cerebro-spinal fluid (the fluid around the brain and spine) a deficiency of two chemicals. These are normally present in quite large quantities in the brain, and in particular in one set of structures in this organ.

The structures concerned are spread around various parts of the brain, but are linked in the form of a circuit. This circuit is called the *limbic system.*

The limbic system controls a lot of the body's processes, such as sleeping–waking cycles, temperature control, temper control, eating patterns and hormones; every hormone in the body is directly or indirectly under the control of the limbic system. It keeps all of these functions in balance with each other.

Any electrical engineer reading this book will know of the concept of a 'reverberating circuit'. You find one of these at the core of any complex machine. For example, if a jumbo jet runs into a side wind, the pilot has to turn the tail flap to compensate, but this then means that the attitude of the wing flaps has to be changed to compensate to prevent the plane falling out of the air. This in turn will affect the thrust required from the engines, and so on. So one change has knock-on implications for a host of different parts of the plane, far removed from each other. Something is required to orchestrate the functioning of the whole machine to compensate for changes and keep the various different parts and functions in balance. That something is a reverberating circuit, which is an electrical circuit with lots of inputs and outputs. It enables every part of the machine to 'talk to' every other and compensate appropriately when changes are needed. It is essentially a giant thermostat, controlling many functions at once.

The limbic system is a reverberating circuit. As well as controlling all of the functions I have already mentioned, its most important function is to control mood.

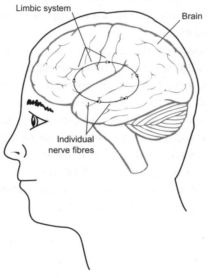

Figure 1 The limbic system

This simplified diagram shows one chain of nerve fibres. The whole system consists of millions of such chains with complex inputs and outputs which are not shown.

It normally does this remarkably well. A human being's mood is usually very stable, given what we all go through, coming back to normal quite quickly after the ups and downs of life. We must exclude bereavement here, which is a separate process, lasting much longer than the normal time it takes for the body to adapt to major events. For everything else, mood returns to normal after a short time. For example, if you win a million pounds on *Who*

Wants to be a Millionaire?, or the Lottery, or the football pools, your mood does indeed rise, for a few days. It then returns to normal, with occasional peaks, mostly in the first few weeks, corresponding with buying your first Ferrari and the like. But at 3.30 on a Tuesday afternoon, a few weeks on, your mood is no different than it was before the life-changing event occurred.

So mood isn't controlled consistently by events or the quality of your life, but by the limbic system. It is this circuit that determines, in the long term, the level of your mood. It is, if you like, the body's 'mood thermostat'.

But like every other system and structure in the body, it has a limit. If you bash a bone hard and consistently enough, it will break. So will the limbic system.

It can be caused to malfunction by a number of different factors. These include viral illnesses such as flu. Most of us have experienced a degree of post-viral depression. It is very unpleasant and debilitating, but normally passes quite quickly. Sometimes it does not and leads to a fully blown clinical depressive episode. Incidentally, don't confuse this with 'chronic fatigue syndrome' or myalgic encephalopathy (ME), which is a separate and very nasty condition, though it also tends to follow viral illnesses.

Other precipitants of limbic system dysfunction are hormonal conditions, illicit drugs, too much alcohol, some prescribed medicines, too many major life changes, too many losses or facing choices involving conflicting needs.

By far the commonest trigger, though, is stress.

Whatever the cause, the end result is the same. If the limbic system is taken beyond its design limits, it will malfunction. The part of it that goes is the gap between the end of one nerve and the beginning of another, or the *synapse*. There are millions of these in the limbic system and they are the most vulnerable part of the circuit. A nerve fibre is essentially a cable. Once a nerve impulse starts down a nerve fibre, it reaches the end without difficulty; the tricky bit is getting the impulse across the synapse. This is done by the first nerve releasing chemicals into the synapse in response to the arrival of an impulse at its end. These chemicals travel across the synapse and when a sufficient quantity of them arrives at the beginning of the next nerve fibre, an impulse is triggered off.

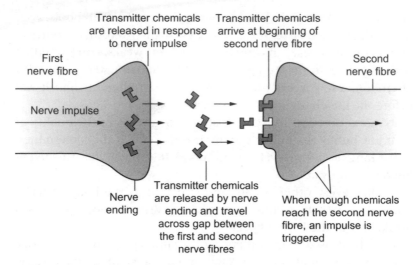

Figure 2 A synapse in the limbic system

Thus the gap is crossed by the nerve impulse and the circuit keeps running.

In clinical depression it is these *transmitter chemicals* which are affected. In response to stress or any of the other triggers, the levels of these chemicals in the synapses of the limbic system plummet (and the nerves probably get less sensitive to the chemicals, too). As yet we don't know for sure why this occurs, but it does, and when it does the circuit which is the limbic system grinds to a halt.

The transmitter chemicals thought to be involved are serotonin and noradrenaline, with two other chemicals, dopamine and the hormone melatonin, more recently discovered also to be in the picture. The truth is we don't know for certain how these chemical and nerve systems work. The more we learn about the limbic system, the more we realize we don't know. Isn't that always the way? Nonetheless, it is still clear that chemical changes in the limbic system are important in development of depression.

When the limbic system malfunctions, a characteristic set of symptoms arises. These symptoms are what define clinical depression and separate it out from other states, such as sadness, disgruntlement or stress. There are some conditions, such as glandular fever, an underactive thyroid gland or ME, in which some of the symptoms are the same and someone under a lot of stress may have some of them; but if you have all or nearly all of them, you have clinical depression. Most of these symptoms are under the heading of 'loss of'. It's pretty much a case of loss of everything – it is as if the whole body shuts down and, as I will outline later, this is possibly what is happening.

Symptoms in clinical depression

Feeling worse in the morning and better as the day goes on. Loss of:

- sleep (usually early morning waking)*
- appetite*
- energy
- enthusiasm
- concentration
- memory
- confidence
- self-esteem
- sex drive
- drive
- enjoyment
- patience
- feelings
- hope
- love
- and almost anything else you can think of.

* These can occasionally be increased, rather than decreased.

The symptom of feeling worse in the morning is a particular 'marker' for depressive illness and is caused by a hormonal change. Under normal circumstances the level of the hormone cortisol fluctuates through the day, with a high peak in the early morning and a gradual falling-off through the day until, by the evening, there is very little in circulation. However, in depressive illness, this morning peak is lost. In some people with depressive illness, other disturbed patterns of cortisol levels occur – and in fact over a 24-hour period cortisol levels in the blood tend to be raised – but in any case the normal fluctuation in levels through the day does not occur and it is this loss of the usual fluctuation, which the body expects, that seems to cause the problem. Thus you feel worse in the morning. This is one demonstration, if there were any doubt, that depressive illness really is physical. There are some researchers who see a rise in cortisol as being more central and even the real cause of depressive illness, disrupting circadian rhythms and thus stopping normal functioning (see Hibernation, p. 28).

The loss of memory experienced by sufferers of this illness is, in fact, apparent rather than real. What actually happens is that you can't concentrate during a depressive episode, so you don't take information in properly. Therefore the information isn't available later to recall, as it hasn't got into the memory store in the first place. In fact, the evidence is that once memories are laid down, they aren't significantly affected by the onset of depression.

One more important fact: depressive illness, or at least the commonest form, which is that caused by stress, nearly always happens to one type of person. So much so, in fact, that it allows me my little party piece in interviews with patients, which is to tell them about their personality before they tell me. Normally, in a psychiatric assessment, one is expected to make enquiries about aspects of the patient's personality. I never bother, because it is nearly always the same. He or she will have the following personality characteristics:

- (moral) strength
- reliability
- diligence
- strong conscience
- strong sense of responsibility
- a tendency to focus on the needs of others before one's own
- sensitivity
- vulnerability to criticism
- self-esteem dependent on the evaluation of others.

This person is the sort to whom you would turn if you had a problem to sort out upon which your house depended. She is a safe pair of hands and you can trust her with your life. Indeed, this person is usually admired, though often somewhat taken for granted by those around her. People are usually very surprised when she gets ill; indeed, she is the last person you would expect to have a breakdown.

But it isn't so surprising when you consider that depressive illness is a physical condition. Think about it; give a set of stresses to someone who is weak, cynical or lazy and he will quickly give up, so he will never get stressed enough to become ill. A strong person, on the other hand, will react to these pressures by trying to overcome them. After all, she has overcome every challenge she has faced in the past through diligence and effort. So she keeps going, absorbing more and more, until, inevitably, symptoms emerge. At this point most people would say, 'Hang on, this is ridiculous, I'm doing too much, I'm getting symptoms! You're going to have to help; it's about time you pulled your weight, and as for you, you're going to have to sort yourself out.' So they pull back from the brink before it is too late. But the sensitive person, without a very solid sense of self-esteem, can't stop struggling, because she fears other people being disappointed in her. Even more than this, she fears being disappointed in herself. So she keeps going, on and on and on, until suddenly: BANG! The fuse blows.

That is what this is: a blown fuse. Again, this isn't a metaphor. The limbic system is a type of fuse mechanism and when it blows, it doesn't matter how hard you try, you can't achieve anything. Once the fuse has blown, you can put 1,000 amps through it, but it won't do any good.

So turn the electricity off.

I will return to this point later, but the point to hold on to now is that you are wrong in thinking you are weak and that you should be ashamed to have contracted this illness. *You have got it because you are too strong.* You are in good company. This is the affliction of the good and the great. These are a handful of those who have suffered from it:

- Oliver Cromwell
- Abraham Lincoln
- Isaac Newton
- Edgar Allan Poe
- Ludwig van Beethoven
- Vincent Van Gogh
- Winston Churchill
- Evelyn Waugh
- Ernest Hemingway
- Tony Hancock.

2

Depressive illness through history

Arguably, clinical depression is the most misunderstood of all illnesses, but our present tendency to stigmatize sufferers is but a pale reflection of what went on in times past. Earliest writings refer to those in an extreme state of withdrawal, many of whom were presumably clinically depressed, as possessed. This demoniacal model runs through ancient Greek literature, though Hippocrates, who was in fact probably an agglomeration of several physicians of the era, emphasized a more humanistic and descriptive approach. He (or they) was the first to describe 'hysteria', a reflection of the fact that symptoms or behaviours can be caused by psychological processes. Roman and Hebrew writers favoured the possession model of mental illnesses and it turns up in the Bible more than once. Throughout Europe, possession by demons and witchcraft was the generally preferred explanation for the changes in a person through depressive illness and other diseases affecting the mind, right up to the middle of the eighteenth century, and in North America later still. Treatment was simple and brutal and was outlined in the *Malleus Malleficarum*, published in 1486. It is not surprising that it took a long time for the condition to be recognized, as there clearly weren't going to be large numbers queueing up to be diagnosed and treated.

In the middle ages, depression was seen as arising from an excess of liver function, leading to a build-up of 'black bile'. The name for the illness stemming from this assumption persisted until very recently. When I was a student, the term 'melancholia' was still in common usage. There is, though, virtually nothing in the literature about the treatment of people with psychological problems of any kind up to 1800, other than by torture. Samuel Proud was one who tried to help. In 1780, though not medically qualified, he treated patients with 'physic and blistering'.

At the end of the nineteenth century things were improving for those treated in asylums, but from available descriptions, only those who were considered a danger to society were offered treatment. A few of these would have been suffering from severe depressive illnesses, but most would have had schizophrenia or severe mental impairment (handicap). It was a German professor of psychiatry, Emil Kraepelin, who first expounded the 'medical model' of psychological conditions, right at the beginning of the twentieth century. He recognized that psychological symptoms such as those of schizophrenia, mania and depression probably had a physical basis, though as yet it wasn't known what that was. This was a gigantic leap towards the concept that those who, by dint of their symptoms, could not contribute to society were ill rather than bad or degenerate. Ironically, when I was learning my trade, in the 1970s and 1980s, the term 'medical model' tended to be used as a term of abuse by some of the more avant-garde therapists to describe the outlook of doctors whom they saw as ignorant pill-pushers. How things go round!

At around the same time as Kraepelin was writing, Freud and his cronies were strutting their stuff. At last someone was coming up with some concepts which could be translated into treatment. Freud did not reject the medical model of psychological disturbance – far from it, he believed that, eventually, a physical basis in the brain would be found for all mental disorders. But he also recognized that psychological and physical processes cannot be separated; the mind resides in the physical structure of the brain. He focussed on what he had, which were powers of observation of human behaviour, and saw that there was clearly more at work than conscious thought. Hence he started working on the part of his patients' mental functioning which was unconscious and related to their basic drives. If he could help them to resolve the conflicts between their drives, whether conscious or unconscious, he postulated that their symptoms would no longer be needed and would resolve. In fact, much of Freud's work was not with people who were suffering from what we would now know as depressive illness, but nonetheless the shift he caused in thinking was immense.

Having said this, even later, between the world wars, there were some methods of treatment in operation which seem pretty odd now. One involved putting patients into a coma by injecting them with insulin. Another, used with people suffering symptoms including depression, caused by syphilis, had them being given malaria.

It was not until after the Second World War that things moved appreciably further forward, helped by chance observations of people suffering from a set of unrelated conditions: epilepsy, tuberculosis and Parkinson's disease.

Electroconvulsive therapy (ECT) arose out of the observation, made earlier, in the 1930s, that people suffering from epilepsy and depression tended to enjoy an improvement in their mood when they were having a spell of particularly frequent fits. The obvious conclusion was to induce seizures in people who wouldn't otherwise suffer from them. They did this initially using injected chemicals and other measures, such as strobe lighting. The most efficient method was found to be passing an electrical current across the temples.

Early treatments were pretty alarming to behold and provided great scope for Hollywood film-makers, such as those that produced *One Flew Over the Cuckoo's Nest*. Sadly, this has left some with the mistaken impression that ECT is still today a brutal treatment, used as a deterrent to wayward patients.

ECT worked. It was the first treatment to make a real difference to those most severely ill people who, by the nature of their symptoms, were unable to engage in any form of talking therapy. Indeed, some unfortunate souls who had been locked away in asylums for years were given a new lease of life.

An even greater advance was the development of antidepressant medications. The first, iproniazid, was being used in the early 1950s as an antituberculous drug on the large TB wards of the time. The patients loved it, as it made them euphoric, but the nurses weren't so keen on manic patients rushing around disrupting their wards, so it was discontinued as an antibiotic. However, when given to depressed patients it had an equally dramatic effect, at least in some. So was born the first class of antidepressants, which are still occasionally used today, the Monoamine Oxidase Inhibitors (MAOIs).

Within a year or so it was noticed that imipramine, a drug used to treat Parkinson's disease (which was also used as an antihistamine), was lifting the mood of depressed Parkinsonian patients in a sustained way, which showed that it wasn't just a stimulant like amphetamine. It was also, incidentally, tried to treat psychotic illnesses, such as schizophrenia, with disappointing results. The treatment of schizophrenia was another therapeutic dawn occurring at the same time, but that is another story.

It was also at around this time that physicians noted that the blood-pressure lowering agent reserpine caused a pattern of symptoms indistinguishable from clinical depression. This drug works by lowering the levels of a transmitter chemical, *noradrenaline*. They put two and two together and suggested that a lack of noradrenaline in parts of the brain might be the cause of the illness. The fact that imipramine increased the levels of noradrenaline available in the very same parts of the brain confirmed the theory. In fact, the drug was found to increase the activity of another transmitter chemical too, *serotonin*. In due course, this chemical was found to be even more important than noradrenaline in depression. Since that time, the science of investigating the actions and the particular parts of particular types of nerve fibre in the brain that these chemicals act upon has become amazingly complex and well beyond me. But the crucial fact that remains clear is that *depressive illness is a chemical condition*.

The advent of imipramine, the first *tricyclic antidepressant*, followed rapidly by amitriptyline and then a raft of others, changed the lives of millions of sufferers of clinical depression, both then and since. Though other drugs, developed since, have fewer side effects, none have been found to be more effective at therapeutic doses. In the majority of cases, clinical depression could now, for the first time, be effectively treated.

More recently, a range of drugs have been developed which are safer, particularly in overdosage, and more acceptable to the majority of patients. The best publicized of these are the SSRIs (Selective Serotonin Reuptake Inhibitors, for what it's worth), which include Prozac. Antidepressant treatments are now not only effective, but usually pretty easy to take.

Meanwhile, psychotherapeutic advances were also continuing. In the 1960s and 1970s *behavioural psychotherapy* was developing. This is based on principles of conditioning. It is a structured and straightforward model, using a variation on the methods used to train an animal. A behavioural psychotherapist isn't interested in your past; it is what you *do*, here and now, which counts. He will teach techniques and direct a change in actions to enable better functioning. Behavioural techniques have been very effective in treating people with anxiety and so have a role in depression, as the two tend to go together, but they are limited in their application to depression itself. I will return to this later.

Psychologists, recognizing the limitations of the behavioural approach, then started looking at the relationship between actions and thoughts. They recognized that depressed people tend to think negatively, and hypothesized that if you could change their way of thinking the illness itself might be influenced, both now and longer term. They were right. It is now accepted that the therapy they developed, *cognitive therapy*, sometimes referred to as *cognitive behavioural therapy*, or *CBT*, is the most commonly effective form of psychotherapy in depressive illness. CBT, added to antidepressant medication, has been shown to be more effective, in many patients, than either treatment used alone.

As I will discuss later, other forms of psychotherapy have probably been unfairly rated as of less use than CBT, simply because their results are more difficult to quantify. My view is that more work should at present be focussing on developing short forms of counselling and exploratory psychotherapy that are practical and cost effective.

So here we are, up to date. The search is on for more effective antidepressants with yet fewer side effects. Sadly, I don't see the same urgency being shown in the search for how to *keep* people well once they have recovered. That requires an integrative view, recognizing that depressive illness has many facets and that, in order to stay well, you have to understand why you got ill in the first place. It also requires of society an effort of understanding and a breadth of view of which I see little sign as yet. In past centuries sufferers were persecuted for being possessed. Now they are merely left to get ill again once the acute episode has been treated. I suppose that is progress.

In order to deal with the illness so that recovery can endure, we need to understand the different ways in which it and its causes can be viewed. I'll have a go at this next.

3

What causes it? Some models and their implications

Everyone has their own take on clinical depression, me included. In the past there were frequent and very boring disputes in the psychiatric press about which causative model of depression was correct. These still occur, but happily less often as clinicians and other groups are recognizing that no single concept says all there is to say about the condition. It's just as well, as listening to a psychopharmacologist and a psychotherapist arguing it out was like witnessing an argument about an object: 'It's green!' asserts one.

'No it isn't, it's round!' protests the other. What they are arguing over is an apple. 'Oh, for goodness sake,' say I, 'someone just get on and eat it.'

All of the models that follow are meaningful for some, and in my view they all have the same end point, which is that if you overload your limbic fuse badly enough or for long enough it will blow. But, and this is the reason for what you might feel is rather a lot of theory in this section, I believe that a crucial part of beating the illness is knowing why you got it in the first place. Each theory has a slightly different set of implications, though with the same end point. Take note of those models and implications that apply the most to you and then take the necessary action.

Let me start with a story, which begins with a little girl (it could just as well be a boy), who we will call Jane.

> Jane is a very privileged child, or at least she seems to be. She has only the best. The best education, meals, toys, clothes, everything. Her parents, successful professional types that they are, have left her materially wanting for nothing. For example, on Christmas Day she is given all the most sought-after presents. But they have forgotten one thing, which is this: the most important thing for children isn't what you do for them, it is what you let

them do for you. When she produces the picture she has been working on for ages at school, shedding glue, paint and glitter, and proudly hands it to her parents, they are dismayed. 'Yes, lovely, dear, but don't make a mess now, put it away tidily and come and open your main present. You'll love it.' Her picture is tossed aside, and with it her sense of worth.

Then she takes her first exam at school. She gives her studies everything. After all, there isn't much of a mark she can make at home, so she might as well. At the end of term she comes home clutching her report, recording that she came top of the class. She expects nothing as she has failed to gain much praise in the past. But her achievement reflects on her parents, so they do take notice. 'Wow, darling, this is brilliant, you're a genius, we're so proud of you!'

From that moment, she's hooked. For the first time in her life she feels important. So next term she works even harder, and as a result she does well again and gets more of the attention she so craves. This goes on and she continues succeeding to the point at which it is assumed she will excel. This is when it gets hard, because while her parents are telling everyone, 'Of course, she will go to Oxford or Cambridge, get a first and have a glittering career,' she is struggling to get through some hurdles which she is finding it increasingly difficult to clear. Because the truth, which has been hidden by her exceptional effort, is that she is only averagely bright. But she grinds on because she has to. She has no other peg for her self-esteem. She gets the results she needs to fulfil her parents' predictions, goes to university, works all hours and gets her first-class honours degree. There is little jubilation now, because her success is assumed by all who know her. She goes on to join a big company, is fast-tracked, and rises rapidly through the ranks. Meanwhile she marries and has a child. Of course, she goes back to work at the earliest possible opportunity.

At this point she faces the dilemma which was always going to arrive sooner or later, because she now has a bunch of people competing with her who are, in truth, more able than she is. She is already working all hours at a hundred miles an hour. Her husband is fed up with her being at work all the time and she is feeling guilty about the lack of time and energy she has for her child. She wants to be the perfect wife and mother as well as the best at her work. In fact, she *has to be.*

She has two choices: fail, or redouble her efforts and, inevitably, break down under the self-imposed strain. But she can't fail; to do so would be worse than death, because she has no other way of feeling worthwhile than through constant success.

She soldiers on with strength and resilience and in the end, sure enough, develops a depressive illness. She has avoided confronting the truth that she is not perfect. 'I would have made Chief Executive, of course, but then I got ill.'

What a price to pay.

You can see very early on someone who is destined to develop clinical depression, once you recognize the pattern. At the time of writing there is an advertisement playing on the television in which Peter O'Toole is dressed first as a wizard, then as a father, and is urging on a small boy dressed in rugby kit. 'Can you overcome your fear, can you catch the wind, can you break through the barriers that confront you? You can, my son, you can!'

Well, of course he can, you silly old fool – he's scared witless of disappointing you. He'll achieve for you and let you take the credit. And later he will get clinically depressed. *Leave him alone and let him learn how to be happy.*

Let's look at some of the other insights that psychologists and psychotherapists have had on this illness. One point, though, before we start. Most psychotherapists don't give instructions, preferring instead to help you in finding your own answers. The instructions here are mine and don't reflect any psychotherapeutic consensus. Indeed, they would see exhortations to change as exactly what they aren't about; there are no wrongs in psychotherapy, only exploration.

Some models from psychoanalytical theory

Overactive superego

In my view Sigmund Freud has received an unfairly bad press. While some of his theories seem strange now, they have often been exaggerated and parodied. He was writing a century ago when the standard treatments for severe depression included being chained to a wall and being doused by high-pressure hoses, or being strapped in a revolving chair and spun rapidly for a protracted period. 'Do you feel better now?' 'Yes, yes, just don't do it again please!' Another therapeutic success.

Freud came into this clinical environment and made some radical assertions, such as: how we are as adults depends on experiences earlier in our lives, and our relationship with our parents determines the way our minds work from then on. These are truisms now but were ground-breaking then, and were possibly the biggest factor in the early part of the twentieth century in moving management of psychological disorder from a custodial to a therapeutic framework.

I will focus on just one of his concepts, that of the superego.

Freud divided the mind into three compartments: the id, the ego and the superego. The id is that primitive part of all of us which consists of drives, unfettered by conscience, such as those to fight, compete for resources, copulate and gain immediate pleasure and gratification. The ego is the central synthesis of all the parts of the mind put together, the self, the 'this is me'. The superego is the conscience, the part which keeps the id in check and keeps us civilized and in control.

These parts of the mind take shape very early on in life. The superego forms through the developing child learning from his parents that there are limits to how far he can go in gratifying his impulses. If his parents are firm but benign, he will develop a sound moral structure but be able later to enjoy life to the full.

But if his parents are harsh, critical and undermining, the poor chap will grow overloaded by inhibitions and self-reproach. It is a sad and ironic fact with which I come face to face all the time that children form powerful attachments to the worst of parents. While the son of a loving and benign mother tends as an adult to give her scant attention, having to be reminded by his wife even to phone his mum on her birthday, the adult offspring of the self-centred tyrant gives her undying love and attention. There was once a comedy series on the TV called *Sorry*, starring Ronnie Corbett, which I had to stop watching because it was too real, too true. Ronnie played Timothy, a 45-year-old man still single and living with his parents. His ghastly mother directed his every action, with cruelly manipulative wit, while his father had long since disappeared to the potting shed to escape her. When Timothy met a nice woman, his mother undermined the relationship to keep her son in her clutches. 'Why do you let her do it?' asks his exasperated girlfriend. He has no answer. In truth, the answer is that his life is one doomed struggle, to gain his mother's love and approval. He will never succeed, because she doesn't see beyond her own needs and wishes. If she had done, he would have grown up confident and outgoing and would have left her long ago.

Another irony is that when parents of this kind die, far from revelling in his freedom, the beleaguered adult offspring takes over their role and becomes ever more self-critical and self-denying. It is as if he carries the critical and undermining parent on his shoulder, telling him all the while that he is no good and deserves nothing. This is his superego and it attacks him constantly. He spends his life focussing on others' needs, and because the users of the world see him coming he soon finds himself with a host of people putting demands on him. Hence the fuse starts to overload.

All models have implications; this one is that you will never be happy and will continue to get ill until you reject the values, statements and assumptions of your critical parent or superego. Do it now and let yourself have time, space and joy. If this makes you feel guilty, so be it. I will discuss later how you can turn your guilt into a useful tool. But change you must, because if nothing changes then everything remains the same, which is hopeless.

Anger turned inward

Most psychodynamic, or exploratory, psychotherapists see depression as anger turned against the self. There are only a few things you can do with anger. You can vent it openly, but that tends to get you into trouble and alienate you from others. You can *sublimate* it: that is, turn it into vigorous action, such as sport, competitive working or artistic endeavour. Many of the most successful exponents in each of these areas are very clearly angry people. You can stop anger building in the first place through balanced assertiveness. Assertiveness in this context is the opposite of aggressiveness. An assertive person quietly but doggedly demands what she needs and makes it clear what is and is not acceptable. For this reason her needs are met and she has no reason to get angry or aggressive. The unassertive person, on the other hand, cannot or will not clearly state his needs. He then fumes when he is neglected, put upon and taken for granted. Eventually the build-up of anger is too much to hold and he explodes in an aggressive outburst. This sometimes happens under the influence of alcohol, and some of my patients deliberately drink to excess because that is the only way they ever get to express their frustration. Sadly, this also tends to lead to a breakdown of relationships.

Another way is to repress your anger: that is, to bury it deep in the back of your brain. People who suffer early adversity learn at a tender age how to do this. At the time this is a necessary skill, but unfortunately it often isn't possible to ditch it later when it becomes counterproductive. Public schoolboys (and girls) of my generation and before exhibit this. I am told by those who should know (our spouses) that we are fine when things are going well. But when the whiff of emotional cordite is in the air, an invisible barrier slams down that is completely impenetrable. The reason is clear. In days past, boarding schools were pretty tough, lonely and savage places. I remember being dropped off at the school at the beginning of my first term and my heart breaking as my parents' car disappeared down the school drive, not to reappear for a month. To an eight-year-old this might as well have been for ever. I have suffered a number of bereavements and other losses since that day, but none compares with the desolation of that moment. In this setting you learn very quickly to hide your feelings, especially of sadness, because any show of vulnerability may be seized upon and used to gain an upper hand in the formation of the pecking order which was a boarding school dormitory. Inevitably, feelings of all sorts get stored up; grief, sadness, shame, fear, loneliness and anger.

Thus is formed the emotionally controlled product of a boarding school education. He seems to remain cool under fire and rarely gets involved in conflictual argument. But the anger has to go somewhere when his environment, for one reason or another, turns hostile. Sometimes it turns inward and is directed against himself. He blames himself for the mounting problems, redoubles his efforts to engineer a solution and starts to overload. While his ego is under attack from his superego, his limbic system begins to creak.

This process can happen to anyone, not just public schoolboys, but is very unlikely to happen to someone who, as a child, has been consistently loved and nurtured. The message for parents is clear: a child doesn't need toughening up. He may seem to be getting tough through a harsh regime, but in fact this strength is an illusion. He is getting weaker and building vulnerabilities for the future. What he needs is lots of love, warmth and cuddles; strength develops through tenderness.

For the adult who recognizes that he tends to repress emotions such as anger, it is worth trying to change the way you operate. I will return to this point later, under the heading of OKness, but for now it is enough to be aware that if you store up your anger or other negative emotions, they are likely to attack you later when things go wrong.

Resonance with past loss

People don't tend to get ill the first time something bad happens. Children, in particular, will seem to cope with whatever you throw at them; they are wonderfully adaptive. For example, a 12-year-old girl who loses her father to cancer will not become obviously depressed. She may become clingy, fretful or poorly behaved for a while, but in due course, if handled well, she will be pretty much back to her old self. There are apparently no problems, other than her missing her dad, for the rest of her childhood. But then twenty years later she is made redundant from her prestigious and well-paid job and rapidly develops a severe depressive illness.

What has happened? Losing your job clearly isn't the same as losing your father. But symbolically there are a lot of parallels. Both involve a shattering of assumptions of security and certainty. Both involve loss of a source of comfort and self-esteem. Both make her feel lost and alone. Her redundancy resonates with her early loss, which had lain dormant for the past twenty years, having been repressed by a child who didn't know how to grieve and was too frightened anyway.

In my view, the way to avoid this descent into depressive illness resulting from resonance with previous adverse events is to take yourself and your feelings seriously. I meet an awful lot of people who, when knocked sideways by a loss or other adverse event, berate themselves for being silly and weak and force themselves to put on a brave face in order to carry on. They struggle on through thick and thin. No prizes for guessing what the result of this is. Better instead to believe your feelings. Think about where they may be coming from, and if possible talk about it to someone you can confide in.

Narcissism

Now here is an unexpected concept to find in a book on depression! Most people think of a narcissist as someone who loves herself, not unreasonably in view of the fable from which the term originates. However, in psychological parlance, a narcissist, far from being in love with herself, in fact hates and despises herself.

Let me take you now into a nursery where a baby is bawling its little eyes out. This has been going on a while. Neither parent hears because they are too busy drinking downstairs. The baby rises to a crescendo of rage and despair and is bright red in the face. This is a terrible noise designed to bring you running. But these parents don't run because they are too sozzled. The baby cries on until it looks as if it will explode, then suddenly it stops.

If you then try to engage the infant with a rattle or other toy, you will find that she will look straight through you, as if you weren't there. You see, she has gone past the stage of rage and despair into a place a psychotherapist colleague has called '*the idle interval*'. This is a mental space past all emotion and hurt. She has tried to interact with the world, but has failed to engage it, so she has had no real choice but to withdraw inside herself.

From time to time as she grows this child will have further attempts at getting something from those around her. Parents, you will be happy to hear, have plenty of chances to engage a child emotionally. You don't have to be a perfectly attentive parent. Indeed, there is some evidence that the best balanced people have been brought up by parents who are only 'good enough', rather than perfect. Ideally, a child should learn that frustration some-times happens; the world isn't always the way you want it. But if you wait, good things will happen in the end.

This child, however, never gets any consistent attention from her boozy parents and so spends increasing time in her own internal world. When she goes to school she has another go. She tries to get attention and approval from her peers by showing off. She hasn't learnt that you get people to like you by showing that you like and are interested in them. Because she is so gauche, she tends to be cruelly rebuffed and so disappears back into her idle interval again for a while, emerging periodically through childhood. But as she isn't interacting in between times, she isn't picking up the same social skills as her peers. Thus each time she tries, increasingly desperately, to get noticed, her efforts are less and less likely to be rewarded. So she remains mostly an insular, unhappy child.

As an adult, this woman is very needy, but doesn't know how to please others. She tends to try too hard and reacts to any reverse or perceived slight by emotionally disappearing again. Thus occupational, recreational and personal relationships fail. She com-pensates by putting ever more effort into everything, while feeling ever more worthless. Then we are on to our familiar path. It is a matter of time before the fuse blows.

If you recognize anything of yourself in this person, the first thing is, in my view, to realize that *it isn't your fault*. Your problems come from your background, not from any failing of yours. Then the key is allowing yourself to pretend. In truth you don't know how to be interested in people, but you need to do the actions of someone who is interested. The reason for this is that people love people who are interested in them.

I hate parties. I tend to get through the worst ones, which are those at which I know nobody, by pretending to be someone I'm not. My most successful role is as a cue-giver. This involves saying nothing at all for the duration of the party other than the sort of facilitatory cues I was taught in my psychotherapy training. These include: 'Really?', 'Gosh!' and 'That's wonderful, you're so brave!' as well as more specific ones such as 'Is that so, even in the south?' After each of these parties I have had feedback that other guests have said to my hosts: 'Isn't he an interesting man, absolutely fascinating.' But I haven't said anything; how can I be so fascinating? The answer is that most people want to be heard and acknowledged.

So if you are just starting to try to get people to notice you, pretend to be interested in them. This isn't deception. As you will see later, your actions will enable you to change as well as inducing the world to be more rewarding to you. And stop trying so hard; you don't need to.

Some models from sociologists and ethologists

Learned helplessness

During my time at medical school we spent a lot of time doing awful things to rats in the name of science. Fortunately this happens much less now. One such cruel experiment has a rat trapped in a cage with a metal grid floor. This grid is linked to an electrical generator, which causes the poor animal to receive a shock every five seconds. The generator in turn is linked to a T-bar mechanism with a timing device attached, such that, when the bar is pressed, the generator is switched off for five seconds.

At first the rat scrabbles around looking for a way out from the cage, with increasing desperation. By chance it steps on the bar occasionally and thus gets spared the odd shock or two. Rats aren't very bright, so it takes quite a while for it to learn that pressing the bar is a good idea. Eventually, however, it makes the link and gets pressing. By trial and error it learns to press at roughly the right frequency to avoid the punishing shocks. By increasing the frequency of the shocks and decreasing the length of respite gained by a bar press you can get the little rodent to expend enough energy to light up a light bulb. Incidentally, you can achieve the same result by rewarding the rat each time it presses the bar. But that's another story and another book. For now let's concentrate on our furry friend trying to avoid punishment.

The rat has now learned the rules and adjusted to them. At this point you play the nastiest trick of all; you unlink the generator from the bar, so the rat can no longer avoid the shocks. At first it assumes it isn't working hard enough and so increases its frequency of pressing. When this doesn't work it races around the cage again trying to find a way out. Eventually it gives up and lies motionless on the floor of the cage.

Then you open the door of the cage. You would expect the rat to leave the shock-giving grid as soon as possible, but it doesn't. It stays curled up on the floor of the cage for some time, before eventually dragging itself slowly out and on to the floor of the laboratory.

Now you introduce into the room a fierce and hungry cat. Under normal circumstances the rat would take this as its cue to beat a hasty retreat. This time it doesn't. It sits passively watching the cat approach and then lets itself be eaten.

Why doesn't it run for it, to save its life? The reason is that you have taught it to be helpless. It has learnt that it doesn't matter what it does, it won't work in the end; there is no point in resistance, it is powerless to affect its environment. It may as well just accept its inevitable fate.

You can teach humans to be helpless too. Let's shift the scene to a room in a house. A little girl is making a Plasticine model of a dog for her dad. She has been good all day and she can't wait for him to get home so she can give him the gift, upon which she has invested much loving care. As she hears her father's car coming down the drive she runs excitedly to the door with her model dog. He enters and she is immediately upon him: 'Dad, Dad, Dad, look, I've made a dog for you, it's lovely and I know you like dogs. It's for you.'

But Dad is very tired and very drunk after a bad day at the office and several jars on the way home to drown his sorrows. Frankly, the last thing he needs now is a screaming kid putting Plasticine and paint all over his suit. He shoves her roughly aside and stomps up the stairs to bed. The little girl reels back, falls over and squashes her model. Tears fall on her wrecked gift and her dashed hopes alike.

The next day she is a little monster, giving her mother a hard time and refusing to do anything she is told. After all, what's the point? Being good didn't get her anywhere, did it! When the time approaches for her father's return, she becomes apprehensive about the consequences in store for her bad behaviour. But when Dad comes through the door, he goes straight up to her, hugs and kisses her and gives her a teddy bear. 'Here's a present for the best little girl in the world,' he says to the stunned child, and feels a lot better. You see, he has been feeling guilty all day about how he treated her the night before, so he is now making it up and he thinks he has made everything all right.

But he hasn't. The child is confused. She thinks: 'Hang on, what's going on here? Yesterday I was really good, made Daddy a lovely model and then he was horrible to me. Today I've been really bad and Daddy is pleased with me. I don't understand.'

This chaotic picture doesn't have to go on for many weeks before this girl learns, 'It doesn't matter what I do. Sometimes nice things will happen to me and sometimes nasty things will, but there's nothing I can do to influence it.'

She has learnt to be helpless.

In the future, as she grows to adulthood, this girl is not going to be good at making choices. She will do what is expected of her and try to fulfil people's expectations, but will ignore her own needs and happiness. She will make few demands on others, but will be vulnerable to the users of the world taking advantage of her good nature. Because she feels powerless to affect her environment, she won't get out of harmful and exploitative working environments, friendships or relationships until it is too late. In the face of unreasonable loads, she will soldier on until . . . and you know the rest.

It is difficult to induce learned helplessness in an adult who has been consistently brought up. It is possible; it has happened to a few victims who I have seen, of major disasters. They teach apprentice torturers to do it in South American dictatorships. The principle is sometimes to reward your victim and sometimes to visit unspeakable torment upon him, but above all, to make him recognize, over a protracted period, that you are in control and that he is powerless to affect his environment.

But it is easy to do it to a child. You don't even have to be intentionally cruel to her. All you have to do is fail to be consistent, so that she doesn't learn that she can make things happen.

If you recognize this little girl in yourself, you may need to look at your assumptions about yourself and your relationship with the world and the people in it. If you assume that you have no choices and that there is nothing you can do to make things better, think again. Talk to any family or friends and see what they think. If you ask for their *real* opinion, you may find that most of them have been clear for ages that you are doing too much, being taken advantage of, in the wrong job, being used by your partner, or the like. Then make some choices, *as if* you felt confident and in control.

Maternal deprivation and attachment

In the 1950s the science of parenting was in full flower. Not only the academic literature, but also the popular press, was full of advice on the dos and don'ts of child rearing. The way that many of these apparently 'evidence-based' directives have now fallen into disrepute should warn us against taking modern research too seriously until it has stood the test of time. I have to say that I don't find many of my colleagues exercising such critical caution.

However, one model from this period, though having a pretty shaky research basis, has generally remained accepted as relevant. This is the concept of 'maternal deprivation'. The child psychologist Bowlby described how the effects of leaving a child for long periods without its mother were, initially, weepiness and withdrawal and, later, retardation of development and poor relationships with peers. Later still, as these children grew to adulthood, they were anxious, excessively needy of love and attention, tending to feelings of anger and vengeance and, as a result of these, they suffered increasing guilt and depression. What the children had been deprived of was their need for *attachment*. This was seen as an evolutionary need, keeping infants, in a hostile environment, close to their mother for protection. Since Bowlby's time it has become recognized that children can manage quite well so long as they have a central, reliable and protective figure, whether this be the mother or someone else.

An adult who has not had her attachment needs met as a child will be over-anxious and needy in relationships, causing her to meet with rejection and loss, leading to more anger, hopelessness and depression (of mood, not depressive illness yet). A vicious cycle is set up with decreasing self-esteem leading to her tending to select partners who are unreliable and unable to meet her needs, and also jobs that won't reward her. She tries to make the unworkable work by trying harder, and so we reach our familiar destination. The onset of depressive illness then makes it likely she will lose her job and her relationship, so yet more attachments are broken. And so it goes on.

Unless, that is, she stops, takes stock, and starts seeking out people, jobs and experiences which will be kind to her. A good place to start is by her being kinder to herself. If she does this, in spite of her instincts, she can develop secure and enduring attachments, which, by this model, are an antidote to the factors which generate depression.

OKness

This is a concept from a school of psychotherapy called transactional analysis. The book *I'm OK, You're OK* (Thomas A. Harris, Pan Paperbacks, 1986) explains it more fully. The concept is a simple one, but, in my view, one with profound importance.

Let me illustrate. I know that I'm not the best psychiatrist on the planet. There are a few I can think of who are truly awesome. Many of them hang around the major teaching hospitals. They are wise, empathic, have read every scientific paper you can think of, have written a lot of them themselves, are universally loved by patients and colleagues alike, have gorgeous spouses, and usually also have a golf handicap of one. They make me want to . . . No, actually, I can cope with them, because while I can't compete with them, I also know that I am a long way from being the worst shrink around either. I know I'm OK. I do the job in my own way as best I can and manage to do some good. That's good enough for me. This is important for my stability, because in my job there are a lot of ups and downs. Occasionally an angry patient tells me I'm no good, should give up and stop messing around with people's lives. While this upsets me, it only does so briefly and I don't lose any sleep over it, because I know what I am. Equally, from time to time, a patient tells me I'm the best thing since sliced bread and should be knighted. While I welcome and encourage such talk, it doesn't essentially alter my self-image, because I know what I am. I'm OK. This allows me to get on with my job unfettered by the need to seek approval, so I can make my judgements objectively in the best interests of my patients.

The reason for this fortunate state of affairs is that, when I was a child, my parents left me in no doubt whatever that I was the most important person in the world. This may have made me into a pretty bumptious and unpleasant adolescent, as I think I was, but over the years the spots get knocked off and now kind friends prick the bubble of my pomposity when it becomes too plain. But what is left from this parental nurturing is an indelible sense that things will be OK, because I am.

So, parents, forget the old maxim. The correct one is: 'Spare the praise and valuing, and spoil the child.'

A lack of OKness is what appears to drive many of my patients to too much effort for too long, in a futile attempt to feel good about themselves. Success and approval for such a person is a drug. The more you get, the more you need, and when you don't get it you feel terrible. This isn't the answer, because the outcome is inevitable and will stop you in your tracks, forcing you to review yourself and the way you operate. Better to do this *before* the fuse blows.

Searching for OKness, if you haven't got it, isn't easy and may require some psychotherapy. However, it may just need talking to friends and (benign) family. Listen to what they say about you, believe it and try acting as if you liked yourself the way they like you. The reason this works is the basic psychological principle that *you become the way that you act.*

This was demonstrated some years ago now in a mid-state of the USA. Two psychologists reacted to reports emerging from the two state psychiatric hospitals that the staff were mistreating the patients. This couldn't be proven as, whenever anybody official inspected the hospital, the staff were as good as gold. So the psychologists therefore determined to get themselves admitted, incognito, one to each hospital, posing as schizophrenic patients. They decided on the delusions and hallucinations they would simulate in advance and went ahead and got admitted as long-term patients. The plan was that, after six months, both of them would emerge at the same time, declare that they were psychologists and present their findings to the world. The trouble was, when the time came, they were both schizophrenic and, as far as I know, remain so to this day.

The same phenomenon lies behind the problem with Ouija boards and the like. Kids get into difficulty with this sort of activity because, if you act bizarrely enough for long enough, you will become bizarre.

This principle is, in my view, central to preventing and emerging from depressive illness resulting from most of the models I have outlined so far. If you want to prevent a depressive episode or stop it recurring once you have recovered, you need to become more OK. To achieve this, you need to start *acting as if* you were OK. The nuts and bolts of how to do this, I will discuss later.

Hibernation

When an animal encounters a hostile environment, it has two choices: carry on regardless, or retreat. Those that chose the former died out long ago. Carrying on searching for food in the teeth of a hard winter leads to starvation. Those of the species that hunker down with a store of nuts in a warm crevice and wait for friendlier times have a chance of survival. Over time, natural selection made these choices automatic, through instinct. Choice was removed by the body developing a physical response to adverse circumstances, leading to the metabolism of the animal slowing to a minimum and it withdrawing to the least challenging place possible. So hibernation developed in some mammals.

While higher primates, human beings included, have learnt to override this process by controlling their environment to a greater or lesser extent, maybe they too can experience the hibernation response. Ethologists (people who study animal behaviour) noticed some time ago that animals exhibiting depressive types of behaviour in response to stress slow their metabolic rates in a similar way to a lower primate entering hibernation. They suggested that maybe depressed humans are hibernating. This model makes sense. Hibernation bears a strong natural selection advantage. Natural selection has stopped. There aren't many things that kill you before child-bearing age nowadays, which is what natural selection works on, so we still have this mechanism, like many others we don't need, such as the appendix, tonsils and (arguably) the fight–flight response. One of the few parts of us that has evolved massively is the brain, which is enormous.

The price we, as humans, pay for the well-developed emotional part of our brains (including parts of the limbic system) may be that, when we experience the physical process of hibernation, we also experience great suffering.

When an animal perceives short-term danger, the hormone adrenaline is released, allowing it to run faster and fight more effectively through physical changes such as raised heart rate, breathing, muscle tension, acuity of senses and such like. If the danger remains for an extended period, the hormone cortisol takes over. This causes a damping down of the immune response (because the body presumes it will be stressed beyond normal limits or injured) and eventually a reduction of metabolic rate, starting the bodily process of hibernation. We know that most of the structures in the brain affected in depression are the same as those involved in hibernation in lower primates, and cortisol levels are raised both in hibernating animals and depressed humans (see earlier).

If clinical depression is the body switching on a protective hibernation response to hostile circumstances, making you stop when your body needs you to, could it be preventing you from developing high blood pressure, heart attacks and strokes in the future? Possibly. More importantly still, could you prevent it happening by appropriate action taken in time? I think so. If you give in and stop soon enough when faced by stresses, you won't get ill.

4

Some models and facts from research on depression

This chapter follows on from the last. Arguably, though, there may be a greater body of research behind these models and their implications for treatment, and for what sufferers need to do to get better and stay well, than for those outlined in the last chapter. You will have gathered from Chapter 3 that I believe that psychiatry and psychology have become rather too obsessed with recent research findings. Research is crucial if treatment of any condition is to advance, but it is only with the sharp light of retrospect that one can differentiate between a piece of research in which the conclusion has been written before the methodology, and that which will prove to influence thought and treatment for a generation and more. The term 'evidence-based medicine' is used as a synonym at present for good practice. In truth, this is a concept developed by politicians mainly to justify not spending money. Many areas of psychiatry are difficult to prove and some of these are expensive. Exploratory psychotherapy is an example. Those that can easily be proved are often over time shown to be worthless. So the insights that I touched on in Chapter 3 are as pertinent as those that follow, though they have less statistical proof to back them up.

Life event research

There was a large amount of this research in the 1970s and 1980s and it confirmed that when bad things happen, particularly over an extended period, both distress and clinical depressions are more likely to occur if these stresses are of certain types. While these conclusions may seem to be truisms, it took a long time for them to be accepted, because there could be more than one reason for an association between depression and life events. In particular it could just be that when someone gets depressive illness, bad things happen to her as a consequence. While there are still one or two psychiatrists who think the link is spurious, the fact that adverse events tend to cause depression is now more or less accepted. Yippee! After forty years we have agreed on the bleeding obvious.

Recent major life events are the first causative factor. Most often, these involve stress, loss, disruption of one's social network, or a prolonged sense of danger, but they can involve any very major change. So divorce or loss of job are frequent culprits, but apparently good changes, if profound enough, such as winning £5 million on the Lottery, are also a risk factor.

Most often, illness occurs if the second causative factor is also present. This is long-term major difficulties. These difficulties involve continuing stressful circumstances which can cause depression themselves or can act together with recent life events to 'tip you over the edge'.

Finally, there are vulnerability factors. These are circumstances which are not enough to cause illness themselves, but do make it likely someone will get clinically depressed if and when a set of adverse life events or major difficulties occur. The first major life event study interviewed every woman in Camberwell; quite a feat. The researchers found three main vulnerability factors to depression in these women. The most potent of these was having three or more children aged five or under. Later research suggests that the kids can be up to 15 and still pose the same risk. The other two risk factors were: having no employment outside the home, and loss of one's mother below the age of 11. Since the first study, others have suggested that anything in one's life which leads to a lack of social support or makes the individual feel trapped, beleaguered and hopeless is a vulnerability factor.

The Camberwell study was focussing largely on women in deprived circumstances. Life for a mother engulfed in screaming kids, with no source of support or relief from the mayhem, is pretty exacting. What I would have liked to know is, what were the mothers who got ill like? I can guess, as the tendency for them to have suffered early loss and be soldiering on without support suggests that they look very much like Jane, from the beginning of Chapter 3.

So it looks as though, in order to get ill, you need predisposing factors in your life, then one or more events or stressful circumstances to act as a 'final straw'. I would add that you also need to respond to this adversity with strength and resilience, in order for the fuse to blow.

You can't escape your past and can't always escape your present circumstances. But you can look for the choices you do have in your life. Put yourself in the equation, together with the kids. Sometimes you will have to find a compromise which isn't ideal for any of you but allows you to carry on doing what you can *sustainably*. It isn't an answer just to deny yourself and focus entirely on others, even your children, as it isn't in anybody's interests for you to get ill.

Cognitive theory

There have been several exponents of this way of looking at depression, the best known being the American psychologist Aaron Beck. Beck looks at a depressive illness the opposite way round from the perspective taken by most psychiatrists. While we tend to see negative and self-deprecatory thinking as being a symptom of the illness, Beck reckons that clinical depression arises from the negative thoughts. If you think negatively, you will have negative experiences, which in turn will lead to a confirmation of your negative views, and so on.

Underlying a set of negative thoughts lie a set of deeply held underlying assumptions that give rise to them. Common underlying assumptions include the following:

- I'm no good.
- It will all go wrong in the end.
- I'm unlovable/nobody will like me.
- I'll be found wanting.
- I have to do more than anybody else to be worthwhile.
- If I'm optimistic, life will play a trick on me.

These underlying assumptions generate the negative thoughts and beliefs which in turn, in Beck's view, cause depressive illness. He classifies these depressive cognitions (or thoughts) as follows:

- Catastrophic thinking: 'A disaster will occur unless I make sure I'm in control of everything all the time.'

- Overgeneralization: 'I got this thing wrong, which means I can never get anything right and so I'm useless.'
- Black and white thinking: 'Things have got to be perfect/I have to be perfect, or else everything is/I am useless.'
- Selective abstraction: 'The positive appraisal I received at work means nothing; my boss criticized one aspect of my last piece of work, so I am obviously despised and will soon be sacked.'
- Personalization: 'The team I worked with didn't get the contract. It is my fault and I have failed unforgivably.'
- Arbitrary inference: 'She just gave me a look which shows she doesn't like me' (despite the fact that she has never suggested anything of the kind).

Beck sees the problem as stemming from a *cognitive triad*, comprising a negative view of yourself, the world and the future. Once you have formed your view of the world, your experiences tend to fit into it, or in the words of a Simon and Garfunkel song, you hear what you want to hear and disregard the rest.

The poor chap looking so sad in the picture on page 33 assumes his boss doesn't like or respect him. As he approaches his superior, the latter looks the other way. 'It's because I'm not good enough,' he thinks, ignoring the fact he won 'top employee' only last month. In fact, the boss hasn't noticed him because he is glancing at his watch. Our cognitively challenged subject then spends the rest of the day worrying about what he has done to upset the boss. He determines to work twice as hard to ensure that his failing, whatever it might be, doesn't happen again. When someone tells him the company's profits have fallen, he assumes he will be the first to be made redundant. He works still harder until he is so exhausted that he starts making mistakes. When these are pointed out, he feels that his worst fears have been realized. He knows of only one way to react, which is to put in more of what he hasn't got: effort and energy. The blown fuse is just around the corner.

I will come to the issue of how cognitive behavioural therapists deal with these distortions later. For now it is enough just to be vigilant about your thinking. Challenge your own negative thoughts. If you find it difficult to do this, have a think about how your most clear-thinking friend or colleague would interpret the situation. You will usually have a pretty good idea of what they would say in this situation. In the one described above they would probably say something along the lines of: 'I don't know, the old man was probably preoccupied, maybe he was thinking about something else.' Now weigh up their explanations against yours and decide which makes more sense. Talk to more than one friend if you need to.

I often tell patients, after a few sessions, to imagine me in miniature sitting on their shoulder commenting on events that worry them. The most reasonable explanation for most events is fairly obvious if you get into the habit of thinking accurately.

I don't personally go for *positive* thinking, which seems to me to be a device for persuading people to do things that they would do better to leave well alone. A rugby coach persuades his team of puny weeds that they can take on the local 7-ft warriors. I'm sorry, you're going to get badly hurt, why not try bowls? No, positive thinking only leads to disillusionment. What works is *realistic* thinking. Aim for this. And above all, notice the good things that happen all the time and are all around you.

One more thing. I believe that Western societies are obsessed with success and that this underpins a lot of our negative thinking. Actually, anybody can succeed; it's easy. All you do is restrict your sphere of activity so that you only get involved in things you know you will achieve. It's a pretty restricted life, but a successful one.

Now, what's really hard but correspondingly rewarding is to *fail well*. This means taking on a range of tasks, experiences and challenges, understanding that you will win some and lose some, forgiving yourself for your failures and learning from them. This way you develop a life that is rich in texture and free from fear.

A few years ago some friends took me to the south coast to try wind-surfing. I had never done it before, but they were experienced surfers. Through the day I struggled to get up on the board and get moving and only managed a few seconds at a time before falling in again, to the increasing merriment of my friends and to my mounting frustration. There was one other beginner there who achieved even less than I did, never once getting upright on the board. At the end of the day I commiserated: 'What a waste of time, you'll not be seeing me doing that again; how about you?' 'Oh, yeah, it was great,' he replied. 'I'm going to give it another go tomorrow.' I asked if he was embarrassed at falling off so much when there were so many good surfers around. He wasn't.

The next year I happened to meet with my friends at the same location, this time having established my role as spectator only. As we arrived, I saw the same guy, windsurfing. He was really good. While I had succeeded in avoiding failure, he had embraced it, with the result that he had a new skill, at which he was clearly having a great time. *In order to achieve success that is worthwhile and wide-ranging, you must first learn to fail well.* Every happy person I have met has achieved this. It doesn't, though, mean making your life a struggle to achieve the impossible.

Cognitive dissonance

This model is not so much about the way you think as about your acceptance of yourself as you really are. The term refers to the size of the gap between your real self and your ideal self.

The poor chap on page 36 is trying to develop a body like Superman, because he thinks that he will be loved and admired if he does so.

Cognitive dissonance

Sorry, mate, you've got no chance. You're a weedy little bloke and you won't succeed if you pump weights around the clock from now till you die. All you'll achieve is frustration, a bad back and, likely as not, a depressive illness. But look, you're a good guy, fun to be with and your friends and family love you. Develop those aspects of your life and enjoy them. Don't try to be what you're not.

It isn't hard to see how cognitive dissonance leads to a blown fuse. If you feel you aren't the way you want to be, the tendency is to strive harder. If your cognitive dissonance is combined with mental strength, determination and persistence, you'll keep trying till your body gives up. That's depressive illness.

That excellent organization Alcoholics Anonymous gets it right in their serenity prayer, which asks for *the strength to change what I can change, the serenity to accept what I cannot, and the wisdom to know the difference.* I would add, look at what you've got and don't forget to develop it, maximize it and, most of all, enjoy it.

Mindfulness research

Not only does depression tend to make you dwell on negative aspects of your life, circumstances, environment and future, but those who focus on the negatives tend to develop depressive illness more commonly than the rest of us. They tend to engage more in self-recrimination for past mistakes and in what might go wrong tomorrow or next year. They usually want to put everything right for everyone, including themselves, and are intolerant of symptoms, particularly anxiety and insomnia, which of course go hand in hand with stress and depression anyway. They are inclined to do battle with their symptoms rather than just allowing and experiencing them. After all, strong people overcome everything, don't they?

It isn't anxiety, or fear, that is the worst thing for worriers; it is the *fear of fear*. If you spend your life worrying about the past, the future and your symptoms for long enough, eventually, when there is enough to worry about, you will blow a fuse and develop a depressive illness.

Eckhart Tolle, the author of the book *The Power of Now* (see pp. 90, 116), realized this. He dealt with his depression by giving everything up (and I mean everything he had, money, friends, property, the lot) and living rough for a period, thinking, and discovering from his uncluttered introspection that unhappiness and stress come not from your circumstances or what happens to you, but from spending too much of your life in miserable self-recrimination for past perceived mistakes and in fear of loss in the future.

Genetics

The degree to which depressive illness, of the kind considered in this book, is genetically inherited is difficult to quantify for sure. However, it is clear that it isn't nearly as strongly inherited as manic depressive illness (bipolar affective disorder), which involves repeated swings from extreme elation to deep depression.

For 'unipolar' clinical depression – that is, depression without the intervening extreme highs – the prevalence (that is, the proportion of the population affected at any one time) is around 2–3 per cent. The lifetime risk of developing the condition may be around

6 per cent. However, this figure varies depending on the definition used and the cut-off point between normality and illness. Women experience this more frequently than do men, though the sexes are coming together in this regard.

If you have one parent who has suffered from the illness, your chances of getting the illness rise to 10–15 per cent. If you have a non-identical twin with it, your risk is in the same range, but if you are the identical twin of a sufferer, your risk rises to around 60 per cent.

So there clearly is a genetic link, but it is nothing like as strong as for some characteristics, like eye colour. If the condition were totally inherited, after all, identical twins of affected individuals would have a 100-per-cent risk. It is also not clear what is inherited here. It certainly doesn't follow, if you have a strong family history of depression, that you are destined to get the disease. This matter has not yet been fully researched, mainly, in my view, because researchers haven't properly separated out stress-induced clinical depression, of the type I am discussing, from a raft of other types and causes of lowered mood.

My intuition is that what is inherited is mostly your personality. As I have outlined, depressive illness tends to happen to one type of person. This doesn't mean that if you have that type of personality you are bound to get depressed; far from it. These traits of strength, diligence and sensitivity can serve you well if used wisely. If I am right, you only get the illness if you let your personality cause you to do too much, for too long, in the face of adversity.

So there is no need for you or your children to get clinical depression, as long as you and they *act* with moderation, maybe in spite of your makeup.

So, that's about it for the models of how depressive illness develops, or at least the plausible ones with which I'm familiar. How did yours develop? Take note of the implications and act on them.

If it seems that most of these models have a lot in common, they do. My point is that they have the same end point – that is, the blown fuse – and so whichever model applies most to you, some of the implications are the same. I have touched on them already and will come back to them in Chapter 9.

5

What to do when you get ill

Whatever your background and whichever route or routes you have taken into clinical depression, I invite you to consider the following: you have done too much, been too strong and tried too hard for too long. Now the fuse has blown. *It isn't your fault.* Far from it: you are worthy of praise and admiration, not the self-criticism that you have been heaping on your own head for some time.

Rest

But first you must give up the struggle. While you continue pushing yourself the body can't start to heal. It's a waste of time, anyway. You can't achieve much because your concentration, energy and judgement are at an all-time low. So stop. This means taking time off work if this is at all possible. It means getting help at home with the kids and domestic chores. It means cancelling all those social events you have been dreading. You are dreading them because you are well aware (your body is telling you) that *they will hurt you.* If you force yourself to endure them you will get worse. It means telling family, friends, your local charity and anyone else you do things for, that they are going to have to do without you for a while. If they complain, get them to read Chapter 1 and this one. Above all, ignore those who tell you to get more active and to pull yourself together, unless you want to be rude to them; that would be fine.

The trouble is that, if you just sit in a chair all day, you have far too much time to ruminate. You worry about all the things you haven't done, all the things that could go wrong and the effect your period of illness will have on your career, family and relationships. This is stressful and so is harmful. Going to bed isn't the answer. Even if you don't simply lie there ruminating and fall asleep, this just makes your already curtailed sleep pattern at night even worse. Your sleep requirement in clinical depression is reduced anyway and any sleeping you do during the day will be subtracted from the hours you are likely to sleep at night. The early hours of the morning, which is when you tend to wake when clinically depressed, is a pretty grim and lonely time to be alone with your depressive ruminations. So there is a dilemma: how to stop yourself ruminating while not overusing your body's scant resources. In my experience, the average person in the pits of a depressive illness has no more than about 10–15 minutes of available energy for anything at all demanding before she gets tired. If she goes beyond this limit on a regular basis, she doesn't get better.

The answers are to find any way that you can of keeping your brain just idling, to avoid any challenging activities wherever possible and to do what you have to in very small chunks. Best of all, be passive. The ideal would be an undiluted diet of Australian soap operas, if you can stomach that sort of thing. They allow you to sit and not to ruminate – a sort of mental wallpaper, filling up the space and covering over the cracks. Meanwhile, you can imitate a vegetable and allow your body to proceed with the task of healing. It will do this so long as you leave it alone to get on with it. If you can't do TV, then anything that you find easy to do. But beware; what you normally find easy may now be difficult. Take things as you find them now and avoid value judgements of the 'oh, that's pathetic, I can't even . . .' type. Look for things that allow you to coast along in neutral.

Don't make any major life-altering decisions at this stage, especially ones that are potentially irrevocable. It's a bad idea for you to resign from your job at this stage, though this may well be a good idea later. Don't leave home. Don't sell anything and don't cancel your holiday abroad yet. You may be better quicker than you think. And *don't harm yourself*. I know it seems hopeless now but *it will all look very different in a little while* when you get better. Yes, you will get better. People recover from clinical depression. Don't punish yourself. Your feelings of guilt are a symptom of your illness and are very unlikely to be deserved. Yes, your illness may have affected your family, but *it isn't your fault*, any more than if you had developed pneumonia. If you were lying in bed wheezing and puffing with a severe chest infection, you wouldn't be berating yourself, would you? You also wouldn't be urging yourself to get on and pull yourself together. This is a much worse illness, while it lasts, than double pneumonia and is every bit as physical. *So get off your case and let yourself be.*

Your spouse may well be struggling with your illness. That is understandable; it is tough living with someone suffering from clinical depression, though not half as tough as having it yourself. You are victims of this misfortune together, with no one at fault. Try to show each other some compassion. Don't make any conclusions about your impotence or loss of sex drive. It is down to the illness, and everything will come back to normal eventually, though it may take a while owing to the medication (see later).

One of the worst symptoms, which makes you feel even more guilty, is loss of feelings for loved ones. Try not to worry; it will all come back. You haven't really lost your feelings; this is just a symptom.

Medication

One of the most difficult parts of my job is often persuading patients who desperately need it to take antidepressant medication. The commonly cited reasons for declining are as follows:

- *'I prefer to do it on my own, without resorting to pills.'* Why? Would you say the same if you had pneumonia? Chest infections, like clinical depression, may recover without medication, but choosing not to take antibiotics is risky and means you will remain ill for longer than you need to. In any case, what are you trying to prove? How resourceful and strong you are? You've already proven that by becoming ill in the first place.

- *'Antidepressants aren't natural.'* No, they aren't, but what's your point? Are you suggesting that synthetic products are, by their nature, unsafe? Or do you mean that naturally occurring substances are necessarily safe? OK, then I'll drink the Coca-Cola while you drink the petrol. Naturally occurring substances are among the most toxic drugs in our pharmacopoeia, such as warfarin, for example, used to treat blood clots but also the active ingredient in rat poison. In psychiatry, the most potentially toxic drug we use is lithium carbonate, a naturally occuring salt that you can mine out of the ground, which is used as a mood stabilizer (see later). This isn't to say warfarin and lithium are bad drugs. They are both crucially important in their own fields and fine if used as they should be; you just have to use them with care. But forget the idea that natural is best; it's bunkum.

- *'Antidepressants are addictive.'* No they aren't. You can get reliant on them if you take them for too long, but that is true of anything and doesn't mean the same as addiction. Occasionally, people who stop their medication abruptly can get withdrawal symptoms, but that just means you should stop your medication as advised by your doctor, in a gradual manner. Very few people have problems on withdrawal if they do this. An addictive drug is one which causes withdrawal symptoms on stopping. But it also loses its effect over time unless the dose is escalated and it causes the person taking it to crave more of it. Antidepressant drugs don't have these properties.

- *'Antidepressants give you a false high and change your personality.'* No they don't. At best an antidepressant can bring the level of the transmitter chemicals in your limbic system back to normal. Excluding those people with manic depressive illness and rare cases when an overshoot occurs, there is a run-off mechanism in the brain which stops the levels of the chemicals getting too high. It is as if the level of the transmitter chemicals was the level of water in a bath. In depressive illness the taps get bunged up and only trickle water in. The bath stays empty as the plug is out. Antidepressant medication puts the plug in. The right level of water is at the top of the bath. Though it takes a while, even a tap running at a trickle will fill the bath eventually. The bath can't get any more than full, because once the level of water reaches the top, it pours over the edge. There is a run-off mechanism in the limbic system such that the levels of the transmitter chemicals can't get any higher than the right level for you. So you won't get a false high; at best antidepressants will bring your mood back to *your normal*. Forget anything you've read saying you can use Prozac as a party drug; you can't.

- *'I've read that Prozac can make you violent.'* Strangely, about two years ago, I read two newspaper articles about Prozac in the same week. One hailed it as a wonder drug. It outlined how this panacea makes you more creative, nicer to be with and generally

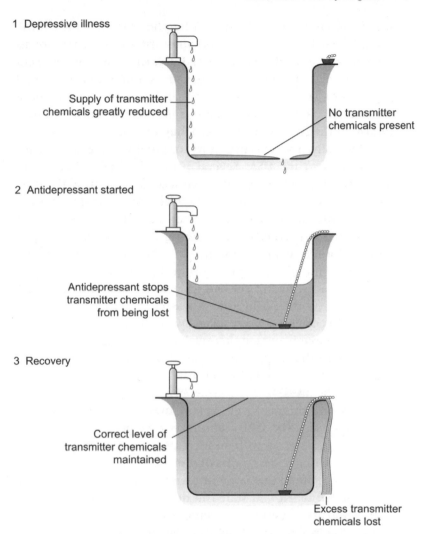

1 Depressive illness

Supply of transmitter
chemicals greatly reduced

No transmitter
chemicals present

2 Antidepressant started

Antidepressant stops
transmitter chemicals
from being lost

3 Recovery

Correct level of
transmitter chemicals
maintained

Excess transmitter
chemicals lost

Figure 3 How antidepressants work

a better and kinder person. It concluded that everyone should be
on Prozac, and that if it were put into the world's water supplies,
there would be no more wars. Well, I ask you, what a load of tripe.
The fact is that, if you give Prozac to someone who isn't clinically
depressed, it will make no difference to their mood or behaviour
whatever. The other article called for Prozac to be banned. It suggested that it turned gentle people into murdering psychopaths

who go around chopping up their families. Oh, give me a break! Look, Prozac is an ordinary antidepressant; quite a good one for some people, as I will describe later, but it isn't a wonder drug and it isn't a devil's potion. Newspapers dream up sensations to sell papers and, having talked to friends and colleagues from around the world, I have no doubt that our press is the worst and most cynical in the civilized world (see Chapter 11).

Incidentally, the violence story originally came from a few case reports in the USA. Several people had been found who had been involved in violent crime soon after starting the drug. However, if you think about it, there are lots of simple explanations for this. An analysis of these cases in retrospect shows that the subjects concerned were suffering from a severe and quite unusual form of depressive illness in which they were suffering delusions (false ideas) of persecution. In the first week or so of taking Prozac, it hadn't yet had time to work, and these people were acting on their delusions. It wasn't the Prozac; it was their illness. This drug has been taken by millions of people. If you look hard enough and employ selective reporting, you are going to be able to show, apparently, that it makes you stand on your head and wear a daffodil in your ear.

Beware the press.

Having said this, as I will explain later, Prozac, like the other drugs in its class (the SSRIs) can make some people feel worse for the first 10 days or so, with an increase in anxiety and agitation. It is possible that some reports of violence in people taking these drugs may relate to this fairly uncommon side effect. If you feel very agitated when you start the drug, get in touch with your doctor and if necessary, stop taking it. Very occasionally, too rapid a rise in serotonin level can lead to a rise in pulse, blood pressure and temperature, with severe agitation. In this situation the drug needs to be stopped and medical attention sought, but a moderate increase in anxiety early in treatment is nothing to be anxious about(!). It will pass.

Teenagers may be at greater risk of self-harm and even occasionally suicide in the early days of treatment. The decision to start these drugs in this age group therefore has to be weighed up very carefully.

- *'I tried an antidepressant for a few days before and it made me feel worse.'* That's because you didn't take it for long enough. Side effects are at their worst in the first couple of weeks of treatment, then generally fade away (though a few may persist – see later). The beneficial effects don't usually start until around two weeks into treatment and it may take six weeks or longer for the full benefits of the drug to be felt. Try again and, this time, persist if you can. If the side effects are too bad, go back to your doctor and tell her. She will change you to a different type of drug with which you will probably have a much better time.
- *'I've tried one for several weeks before and it didn't work.'* OK, you've given it a fair try, but it may have needed an increase in dosage. Around 50 per cent of people who respond to an antidepressant need an increase in the starting dose a few weeks into treatment.

  Nearly 70 per cent of people with real clinical depression will respond to the first antidepressant they go on, if they tolerate it and the dosage is got right. But each type of drug covers a different 70 per cent and no drug is successful for everybody. So if one antidepressant doesn't suit, don't give up; try another. It's odds on it'll work.
- *'I looked at the patient information leaflet (PIL) that came with my tablets and the list of side effects scared me so much that I decided not to take them.'* These leaflets are the bane of my life. I'll bet it was a politician who decided on them. Like the other political

'improvements' to the health service, they have done untold harm. The PIL has to list every significant side effect that has been described anywhere in the world, even once. You're about as likely to suffer from some of them as you are to win the National Lottery. But there they are, and many of my patients assume they are going to get all of them, including 'collapse, heart failure and death'. No you won't, but do read the leaflet and if you get any worrying side effects, go and talk to your doctor about them. If you looked at a PIL for paracetamol you would find it terrifying, but most of us use it from time to time. Medications are pretty safe if you take them sensibly; certainly a lot safer than leaving your illness untreated.

Psychotherapy

Sadly, this is a shortage area in the health service. While I blame politicians for most of the ills of the NHS, this one isn't their fault; well, not entirely. Psychotherapy is expensive and labour inten- sive. In my view most people suffering from depressive illness can benefit from psychotherapy of one kind or another, but if everyone were to receive it the entire staff of the NHS would have to retrain as psychotherapists and there would be no funds available to treat anything else. We have to be selective and, mostly, concentrate on those therapies that are brief and focussed. It is nowadays polit- ically incorrect to suggest that one should seek treatment outside the health service – but, never one to miss an opportunity to offend, I'm going to suggest it. Only, though, if the therapy you need isn't available under the NHS, within a sensible time. In many of the trusts around my neck of the woods, you will wait for over a year for exploratory psychotherapy. I'm sorry, but that's just silly; it isn't a service, it's a pretend service. Why not be honest and just say: 'Sorry, we can't provide exploratory psychotherapy; it's too expensive'? That's OK, we understand; this is the real world. But if you are going to do something, do it properly and don't have people hanging around for 18 months when their crises and issues are alive and accessible *now*. Check out your local trust, but if you want an in-depth psychotherapeutic exploration, you may need to consider paying for it, if this is feasible.

Most people don't need long-term exploratory psychotherapy. Considering the models in this book and working on the implications they contain may well be enough. If it isn't, there are four forms of therapy which will probably be fairly accessible locally under the NHS. These are *supportive counselling, group psychotherapy, short-term focal psychotherapy* and *cognitive behavioural therapy (CBT)*.

I'll go into these therapies in more detail later. For now, just a brief description of each. Supportive counselling is not seeking to explore any background or make any very profound changes, beyond those necessary to allow you time and space to heal. It seeks to build up your defences against the problems surrounding you, by talking things through. Most members of the community mental health team can do this work and counsellors are available in many General Practice surgeries.

Group psychotherapy comes in lots of different forms. Most psychiatric day hospitals and community mental health resource centres have a range of available group activities, all the way from simple relaxation training to fully fledged cognitive behavioural therapy or sometimes even exploratory psychotherapy. Many people have a natural reluctance to sharing their problems in public, but if any group sessions are recommended to you, consider them seriously. You are likely to find a lot of wisdom, practical advice and skills to help you cope, and people who think like you in these groups.

Short-term focal therapy does exactly what it says on the tin. It doesn't seek to dig into the past, except in order to understand your present conflicts and why these stresses are making you ill now. It seeks solutions to your present problems, rather than working through a lot of issues from the past. It usually involves a session with a therapist once a week, or fortnight, for a few months.

Cognitive behavioural therapy looks, here and now, at the way you think and tries to change your negative and self-defeating thinking patterns through challenging them. More of this later.

The bottom line is this. Antidepressants and rest can get you better, but if nothing changes it's a matter of time before you get ill again. If you can change the way you operate, so that you are part of the equation rather than just a tool for others to use, there is no need to get a further episode of depressive illness. If you can't, you probably need some form of psychotherapy.

6

Recovery

There you are, I told you that you would start to feel better eventually. Sometimes it happens quickly and sometimes it takes longer, with one or more changes of treatment along the way. But, in the vast majority, it happens.

Now, this is where it gets a bit complicated. Recovery isn't, unless you are very lucky, a smooth path upward. If you try to hurry yourself to full recovery, the process can be very turbulent indeed and take an age. If you do everything right, there are still usually a lot of ups and downs along the way, but they are minimized. Presuming you follow my advice, you can expect a pattern of recovery something like that shown in Figure 4.

The graph shows the pattern of recovery of just one symptom of clinical depression: depression of mood. The other symptoms tend to follow the same basic pattern, but the timing varies from symptom to symptom in an unpredictable way. One person may

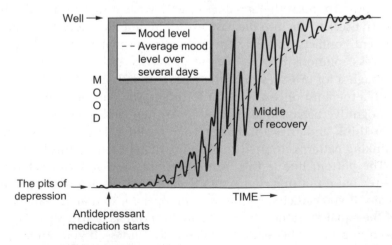

Figure 4 Graph of recovery of mood versus time

find that her mood improves first, but it takes ages for her sleep to recover, while for another it is the other way round, with his depressed mood being the last symptom to lift.

As you can see from the graph, it takes a while for anything to happen after you start taking the antidepressant. Then you get the odd slightly better day. But not much and not often; most days are still a torment. As time goes on, though, the fluctuations get larger, until, in the middle of recovery, the swings day to day are enormous. One day you feel almost back to normal, then the next you feel as bad as ever. A sad fact is that the commonest time for a person to take his life is not when he is in the pits of depression, but at this point, when he is beginning to get better. One reason for this is that, when you have had a really good day, the bad day that follows is thrown into sharp relief and so seems even worse than the gloom of the days when every day was bad. The other is that, if you happen to be someone for whom energy and volition come back before mood improves, there is a risk of you getting the where-withal to carry through self-destructive thoughts that you have had for some time, but not had the energy to act upon.

The crucial message at this time is: *don't act; you are going to be better soon; this is only a bad day.*

As time goes on the fluctuations in mood again lessen. The bad days get less bad, less frequent, shorter than a whole day, and even-tually peter out altogether, though you can sometimes be surprised by a rotten one quite late in the process.

Looking at this graph in retrospect you can see a pattern, involving essentially a steady march towards full recovery, with a lot of background 'noise'. But when you are in the middle of it you can see no such pattern. You are assailed by enormous fluctuations in your mood day to day, with no clear direction. It is crucial not to over-react to these fluctuations. The tendency, on the good days, is to assume that you have recovered. 'That's it, I feel better, I'll just get on now and put it all behind me. My problems are over.' *No they're not, not yet.* The next day, particularly if you have taken advantage of the surge of energy you had yesterday to rush around doing things and sorting things out, you have a particularly black mood and feel as bad as ever. 'Oh, no!' you wail, 'it was all an illu-sion, I'm not getting better, I'll never recover, it's all hopeless, I'll be like this for ever.' *No you won't, it's only a bad day; this is normal recovery. Tomorrow or the next day will be better.*

If you over-react to the normal fluctuations of recovery in this way, you can slow the process a lot, so don't. Instead, enjoy the good days, but be careful not to overdo it. On the bad days, just accept them and wait for tomorrow in the knowledge that further good days will come with ever increasing frequency as time goes on.

So how much can you do at any particular point in the recovery process? The truth is, I haven't the faintest idea, but you do *because your body tells you*. If you overdo it physically, your body starts feeling heavy and lethargic, as if wading through treacle. If you overdo it mentally, you start not being able to think straight and you can read the same page of a book three times without being aware of a word that was written. If you overdo it socially, you will have spoken to someone for five minutes without knowing what subject is being discussed.

If you keep going past the point of these warning signs, you will, sure as eggs is eggs, have a rotten day tomorrow. If you repeatedly do so, you experience the yo-yo effect. On good days, fired up by enthusiasm, you determine to catch up on all those tasks you had been unable to complete through the illness. You ignore the cues your body gives you after ten minutes telling you that you are tired and should stop. 'That's ridiculous,' you tell yourself, 'I can't be tired already; I've only done ten minutes. I can usually go on for hours. I'll just keep going.' So you carry on, through the barrier of tiredness.

From this moment, you have condemned yourself to a rotten 36 hours (or up to 72 hours if you overdo it grossly). Your body goes back into shut-down, forcing you to rest the next day (or three). This is all that is needed for healing to resume, so you then have another good day, which you use to rush around again. Another bad day follows and so on, and on and on.

If you do it this way, recovery can take an age.

Much better to do what your body tells you. You will get better quickest if you listen to what it says. It gives you all the data you need. Yes, I know this can be very difficult in the real world, with a family to look after and a mortgage to pay, but it is in everybody's interests for you to take it slowly at this point. After all, if you suffered a nasty fracture of your leg and were in traction, how would your orthopaedic surgeon respond if you demanded to be allowed to get up and walk after a week?

'But I've got to,' you protest. 'I've got shopping to do, or my family won't eat, and the children have to be taken to school.'

'I'm sorry,' the surgeon replies, 'but if you try to walk now, before your leg is healed, it won't mend and you'll be laid up for longer in the long run.'

'But what am I to do then? My family depend on me.'

'Someone else will have to do these tasks,' she replies, 'your husband, for instance.'

'But he has a demanding job, he's too busy, he can't.'

'Well, someone will have to; you can't and that's final.'

In truth, this sort of discussion rarely happens on an orthopaedic ward, because everyone recognizes that a broken bone has to be given time to heal, and so, somehow, people rally around to make sure that life goes on while you await recovery. This is ironic as depressive illness (or a fracture of the limbic system) is a much more serious condition than a broken leg. After all, the limbic system is a delicate structure made up of nerve fibres, while a bone is a simple and pretty solid structure. The reason for this discrepancy, of course, is that depressive illness isn't usually recognized for what it is. So, just in case you or those around you haven't got the message yet, let me say it, loud and clear, one more time: **Clinical depression is a physical illness and you have to take it seriously**.

So how do you start getting more active once recovery starts?

After all, if you never increase your level of activity, you'll be feeling fine, but doing nothing, a year from now. The answer is that you start by doing bits of things. The key is to do what you've never in your life done before, which is to start tasks but not to complete them. This will go against the grain, as the illness happens to the completer–finishers of life, but it is essential.

An indication of whether you are getting this stage right I call *'the Hoover in the middle of the room test'*. If I were to come into your house in the early stages of your recovery, I should see a whole set of part-done tasks and the Hoover sitting in the middle of the sitting room floor.

If you have a good day you might feel you would like to do a bit of spring cleaning. So you get the Hoover out. No problem so far; you have to start doing things sometime. You start Hoovering the sitting room, but halfway through, after 15 minutes, you start feeling heavy, tired and lethargic. Now, this is the crucial moment: you *switch off the Hoover and leave it in the middle of the sitting room floor.* You go off for an hour and sit down, watch the television, potter around, or whatever. When you feel your energy coming back, you can do a bit more, but only until you feel tired again, at which point you again stop. By the end of the day you may have done about half the house. Because you have stayed within your body's limits, you may well feel OK the next day and be able to finish the task; if not, then the day after that.

Unfortunately, the sort of people who get this illness, when getting tired, tend to say to themselves: 'I'll just complete the task and then I'll rest.' Too late. By the time you have finished Hoovering the house, you have gone way past your body's capacities at this early stage and have condemned yourself to a rotten 36 to 72 hours.

So don't push yourself; *ease yourself towards recovery at a pace your body can manage.* If you do this you will find that gradually, with some hiccups, you will be able to do more and more. At this point it is worth separating your activities into categories: mental, physical and social. Make sure that you do something mental and something physical every day, and something social every week. But make these activities very moderate and within what your body can manage. If you feel tired, stop. If you have a bad day, have a think:

'What did I do yesterday?' As likely as not, that was too much. So, over time you gather a data bank of what is, and what isn't, too much for you.

This stage is quite complicated. In the pits of depression it's simple: do as little as you can. At full recovery it's simple: you can do, within reason, whatever you like. But in the middle of recovery, it is a constantly shifting process of trial and error. The envelope of how much you can do is continuously expanding, presuming you aren't pushing too hard. If you never get it slightly wrong and end up having a bad day through overdoing it, you may be missing an opportunity of progressing a bit faster. But if you are having lots of bad days through the 'yo-yo' effect, you are pushing the envelope too hard. Act as a scientist, observing your responses and tailoring your activities accordingly. Avoid any extremes. To begin with, a physical activity probably just means a stroll down to the corner shop to buy a newspaper. Don't go to the gym yet, as by the time you have got there and changed you'll probably feel tired and need to come home. That then feels like a failure and lowers your morale unnecessarily. A mental activity may involve reading a few pages of a tabloid newspaper, but not a chapter of a book, as you'll probably feel blank after a couple of pages but be tempted to push on to the end of the chapter. A social activity may mean going out with someone for lunch at a quiet pub, but not being driven by friends to a party, which will lead to you being trapped and unable to leave when, after half an hour or so, you are feeling tired and edgy.

Use your common sense and listen to the messages your body is giving you. They are true. Take your recovery as it is, rather than how you would have it be. You'll be well soon enough; just let it happen.

7

Staying well

If you look at most textbooks on depressive illness, you will read that it is usually a recurrent condition. That is, most people who get an episode go on to have one or more further episodes in the future.

I don't find this to be so. While some people do have recurrent spells of depression, they are in two groups. The first group comprises those who have a recurrent illness which is independent of, and largely unaffected by, stress. As I mentioned in the introduction, I am not dealing with people who have this type of condition here. The second group, which is much the larger, comprises those who get further episodes of clinical depression because they have learnt and changed nothing from their first episode.

If you keep putting 18 amps through a 13-amp fuse, it will keep blowing.

Once you have recovered from an episode of depressive illness, it is possible not only to stay well but also to become happier than you have been for years. In order to achieve this, though, you must understand why you became ill in the first place and then make the necessary changes to put these circumstances right. You must *make choices in your life.*

There are lots of apparently valid reasons not to do this. When I urge a busy businessperson to look at the choices in his life, I tend to get a scornful response: 'Choices, what choices? When you have responsibilities, you have no option but to soldier on; the school fees and the mortgage have to be paid.' But he is wrong. There are changes you can make to your life without changing the children's schools or moving house. These changes won't be easy and will involve learning to say no, and to be more assertive in setting out your needs.

You may remember Jane, from Chapter 3. I once treated a doctor colleague who was very like Jane. We'll call her Sue. She is happy for me to tell her story.

Predictably, Sue was one of the best GPs around. Her patients loved her, as she gave them more time and attention than any of her peers. She rarely said no to her colleagues when asked to take on extra duties. She was also a devoted wife and mother. The story is familiar and, of course, she eventually blew a fuse. I treated her with the usual healing balm of antidepressants and rest. She recovered and returned to her practice. Six months later, having battled away in the same way as ever, she relapsed. More of the same remedy, recovery and another attempt to return to work. This failed for the same reason as before.

Sue and I were forced to accept that it wasn't going to work. With great sadness we took the necessary steps for her to retire on medical grounds. When eventually her retirement happened, her patients and colleagues were very sad, but she was happy. I was confident she would do well as she had made plans to do what she wanted with her retirement.

To my horror, eight months later, she was back, worse than ever. 'What on earth has happened?' I gasped. 'You were doing so well; what went wrong with the lovely retirement you had planned?' It transpired that her colleagues from far and wide had heard about her retirement and had long known of her excellent reputation. They flocked to her in their droves. 'Er, Sue, you couldn't do this clinic for me, could you? We're a partner down at present and rather pushed,' 'Sue, as you've got some time on your hands, could you locum for me while I take some leave?' She was co-opted on to committees at her children's schools and for various charities. Brother, sister and parents all had her running around. Before she could blink, she was doing about twice as much as she had done when in full-time practice. The result was inevitable.

Sue had difficulty saying no to people and so was constantly buffeted by life, unable to make any choices or to take any opportunities to grasp happiness.

Don't be like Sue; you'll be admired if you copy her, but only for a while. Your admirers will turn on you when you can't do it for them any more. They won't be there for you in your hour of need, because they are takers, not givers. Better, right now, to *make choices for yourself* and *take the opportunities that are presented to you*. Some of those around you will grumble; you need to keep an eye on them – they are the takers. Those friends who really care for you will welcome your taking more for yourself. In any case, you need to take responsibility for your own happiness. Don't expect others to make you happy; forge it yourself. If your family are struggling because they have got used to you doing everything for them, understand their distress but leave it to them to work through it. It's their struggle, not yours.

This turning of the worm may create a crisis. I can't tell you the number of times I have successfully treated one spouse, only to have to treat the other soon afterwards. If this leaves me open to a charge of destabilizing their relationship, I cheerfully plead guilty. The ancient Greeks knew this issue well. The word '*crisis*' comes from the Greek, meaning literally '*a time of opportunity*'. Miss the opportunity to destabilize the system you are in now and you condemn yourself to more of what you've had for years. *If nothing changes, everything remains the same.* This time of turmoil is when things can change, if you choose for them to do so. But it will have to be you to do it. Nobody else will; they have become too comfortable with the status quo. Why should they change things when there has always been you to rely on?

Changing things in your favour will make you feel guilty. That's a problem that stops many of my patients in their tracks and prevents them from creating enduring change in their lives.

Well, my friends, I've got news for you: **guilt is good**. In fact it is essential. If a newly recovered patient of mine tells me she is feeling guilty about the changes she is making and the demands

she is putting on to others, I go 'Hurrah!' That means she is making the changes she needs to, in order to forge a life for herself which is sustainable and capable of producing happiness in the long run (for herself *and* those around her). Indeed, perversely, life is going to get better for those close to you, by the fact of you placing limits upon what you choose to do for them. But if guilt is good, resentment is bad. If you find yourself feeling resentment, you are not making the changes you need to or sufficiently asserting yourself.

Imagine depression as a dark room: there is only one way out to the bright garden of health and happiness – and that is through a doorway marked 'Guilt'.

So don't try to avoid feeling guilty. It is a good sign. Anyway, if anybody takes issue with what you are changing, blame it on me; it's no skin off my nose.

Having said this, beware of swinging to extremes. As you will read later, in British culture we have a tendency to do this. Occasionally I see an unassertive, downtrodden spouse swing to become a demanding and aggressive tyrant. The overdiligent business executive who has blown a fuse retires early and withdraws almost entirely from the world. The Mr Dependable starts having affairs and getting drunk. On the surface, these massive changes seem inexplicable, but they are not. In fact, little has changed, because opposites are very similar. Unassertiveness and aggressiveness are

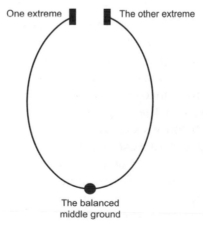

Figure 5 The radical centre

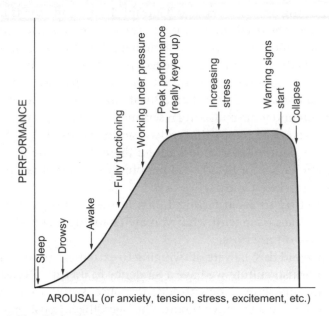

Figure 6 The Yerke-Dodson curve

two sides of the same coin, as are extremes of diligence and laziness, or reliable self-denial and impulsive hedonism. The really radical change is the middle ground, or balance. It is this that you need in order to avoid oscillating from one extreme to another, without enduring change.

As you can see from Figure 5, the extremes are very near to each other and it is only a short hop between the two. The middle ground is the furthest point distant. This is the stable point, which can last. Finding it is a major part of staying well.

I'm not advocating mediocrity here, just sustainability. The key to performing well in the long term without blowing a fuse is operating at just below peak capacity. There is a graph which demonstrates this called the *Yerke-Dodson curve*.

This is a graph of level of performance against level of arousal. I use the term arousal because it implies a scale from very low to very high, but you could just as well call it anxiety, tension, alertness, excitement or stress. They are all different aspects of the same thing.

At zero arousal you are asleep, so you can't do anything. As you wake up you are pretty dozy and can't do much. You've got to be a bit more with it to make breakfast, and to do tasks of any complexity more aroused still. To work effectively in a competitive environment you must be quite aroused. A bit more and you're at your peak, really keyed up, flying, ready for anything. The trouble is, this level is a greasy pole. You either keep going up, or you slide down. The most efficient way of operating is to be just below the peak, rising to this level for brief spells as you need to.

You see this in action in competitive sport. Here are human beings operating at the edge of their capacity for all to see. The best exponent of the brief sally up to the top of the Yerke-Dodson curve was the tennis player Pete Sampras when he was at his peak. At the beginning of a set he was all cool and loose-limbed. He seemed to be strolling around in the park; quite good at the game, just keeping up with his opponent at this level of arousal. Then, at around the seventh game of the set, he stepped up a gear. His whole posture changed; he started bouncing around, his eyes got wider; he looked like a tiger ready to pounce. He would win the game, hold his own serve and before you knew it, he'd won the set. Then he'd be back to lolloping around for a while again. If a match ever went the distance to five sets, which it didn't often, Sampras nearly always used to win, because, while the other guy busted a gut, he had only been fully extended for short periods and had plenty left in the tank.

You achieve more in the long term if you operate at slightly below your peak capacity.

If you try to stay at your peak, you will gradually slide upward, to an increasingly high level of arousal. Now you're running really hot. To use another metaphor, this is the swan on the water; all serenity above, but paddling like heck underneath. Nobody around you realizes there is a problem, but you do and you are beginning to feel the strain.

There is quite a bit of a plateau here, but when the fall-off happens there isn't much warning. Your arousal level goes up and up and up, then – wallop! You fall over the edge and you can't function at all. First time this happens it may take the form of 'losing it': irrational behaviour, running around like a headless chicken, or exploding at someone. It may exhibit as a panic attack, in which you feel extreme fear, breathlessness, palpitations, sweating, light-headedness and a feeling of being separated from the world by a thick pane of glass.

If you get a panic attack, unpleasant though it is, don't panic! It's a normal reaction. Though you may feel as if you're going to have a heart attack and die, take it from me, you won't. The problem isn't your heart, it's that you've been running so hot that your brain is perceiving danger when there isn't any. This happens because the human body is out of date. It's designed for life on the primordial plain millions of years ago. In those days, in order to pass on your genes, you had to be very good at only a few things: fighting, growing crops, procreation, killing wild animals to eat them and avoiding being killed by them. The human body is well adapted for these demands.

If you emerge from your cave to be confronted by a sabre-tooth tiger, you're going to have to react very quickly or you die. Your body, with the aid of the hormone adrenaline, gears up for explosive action with lightning speed. Within a couple of heart beats your muscles are in a state of tension, your heart is pumping faster, you are breathing rapidly, your nerves are all super-sensitive, your senses are hyper-acute and you will experience problems 'at both ends' (to

make you as light as possible, so you can run a bit faster – even a kilogram may be the difference between life and death).

So these changes are highly adaptive to being confronted by a sabre-tooth tiger. But if you're sitting in an office with nowhere to run they are very unpleasant and frightening. They aren't dangerous, but they are a warning to you that you are running too hot.

If you don't change something soon, you're going to fall over the edge of the precipice and not come back up for a much longer time. This is depressive illness. So before you get another episode, pull back, make some changes. Maybe learn a relaxation exercise (see Chapter 10). Above all, don't exist all the time at your limit. Several of my patients, who, as you can imagine, the illness being what it is, include many of the good and the great, tell me that *you can achieve 99 per cent of the output with 60 per cent of the effort.* And it will be sustainable.

In my view it is also important to spend some of your time in pointless activity. If you are all the time doing things that bring tangible results, the chances are that you are running too hot. Why do you have to be useful all the time anyway? What are you trying to prove and to whom? Try making yourself stop, for some time every day and for a longer period at weekends. That's why I play golf. It's difficult, time consuming and completely pointless. I'm not very good and I love it! Being allowed to do something really badly without anybody being upset is a joy. Whatever activity (or inactivity) you use for this purpose, do it badly, if you can. If that is really hard for you to do, I rest my case. But please do it; it's a central part of enduring recovery.

There seems to be so much to change to stay well. There may well be some work to do on what underpinned your overdiligence and excessive strength. That is the province of psychotherapy and I'll return to that later. But for now, I would like to keep it simple. There are just three questions that separate out those of my patients who stay well after recovery from those who fit the stereotype and continue to suffer episodes of illness. They are these:

- *What is it all for?*
- *What do I want?*
- *Where is the balance in my life?*

If these questions sound like ancient Greek to you, you've got a problem; it's a matter of time before you get ill again. If you can answer them, you've got every chance of remaining healthy and, in due course, getting happier than you've been in a long time.

Let me model a set of answers to these pivotal questions (only the second answer is really mine):

- *What is it all for?* I've never thought about it before, but now that I've got ill, I realize that I've been struggling to be great all this time because I assumed I had to. Now I see this leads nowhere other than to exhaustion, irritability, illness and an early grave. My wife doesn't want the big house and car I've strived for; she just wants me to appreciate and love her. The kids avoid me because I'm so tetchy. In fact, if I'm honest, it has been for my dad, to try and impress him and have him approve of me. But he was constitutionally incapable of being impressed by anyone, silly old sod. And he's been dead ten years. Oh dear, I think I missed the point somewhere. But now this illness has given me

the opportunity to understand the point of life before it's too late. Many never gain the privilege of learning this lesson. I'd better decide what I want to do with my hard-earned understanding.

- *What do I want?* To love and be loved, to see my kids become who they can be, to make a bit of a difference in my work and my writing and to achieve a single-figure golf handicap.
- *Where is the balance of my life?* There hasn't been one. In the fight between work and the rest of my life, the ref stopped the bout ages ago to spare the challenger unnecessary punishment. I need to earn enough to keep the kids in their private schools, but the rest is optional. This job makes people ill. Just look at the others in my office. Over a third of them have been off with stress this year and I reckon Phil's 'ME' was really stress. Sarah has gone through a divorce; her husband said he wouldn't recognize her if he saw her in the street. The ones who have stayed well have been a waste of space. You know, I don't think that anyone who really cares and works hard can stay well in this job. I'm off to look at the job pages! In the next one, I'll do the best I can, in the space that is left when I, my family and friends are taken care of.

If your life is a domestic one or you are Queen of England, if you are rich or poor, married or single, straight or gay, the questions are the same. Work out your own answers. Then put them past your best friend (not your spouse). If you get them right, congratulations! You've just won health and, if you're lucky, happiness.

You won't always be happy, of course, because sometimes life throws you some unpleasant ordeals. When it does, be sad. Don't put on a brave face. But be flexible.

In the storm, the stout oak falls, but the bendy reed survives. *Be bendy.*

8

More about treatments – physical treatments

Antidepressant medication

Depressive illness involves a lowering of the levels of the transmitter chemicals in the limbic system and the nerve fibres becoming less sensitive to the chemicals that are left. Antidepressants work by bringing the levels of the chemicals back to normal and making the nerves more sensitive, so that the limbic system starts running again. But there are lots of different antidepressant medications, each with different advantages and disadvantages and some categories working in different ways to others. They are all effective in the majority of people suffering from clinical depression, around 60–70 per cent responding well to any one medication, but each drug covers a slightly different 60–70 per cent. If you're unlucky, you may need to go through a few different types to find the one that does it for you.

The chances are that the first drug you go on will work, so long as you take it for long enough. Remember that side effects are at their worst in the first week or two, while the beneficial effects usually take a few weeks to kick in.

It is crucial that you keep taking the medication once you get well. Patients sometimes stop taking the drug as soon as they feel well. As often as not, they relapse, then losing faith in medication. They come to the erroneous conclusion that, as the illness returned when they stopped the drug, it was only being masked by the medicine. No, the reason for the return of symptoms was that the limbic system hadn't yet had time to heal.

Once the antidepressant brings the chemicals back to their normal levels, it needs to hold them there for a while. It's like suffering a severe fracture of your leg. Once the fracture is reduced, the bone put back into a straight line and encased in a plaster cast,

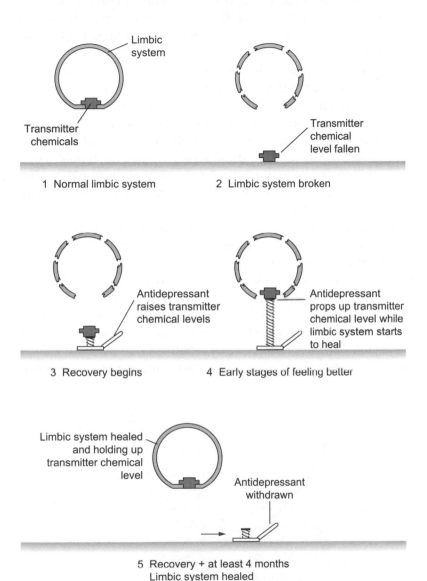

1 Normal limbic system

2 Limbic system broken

3 Recovery begins

4 Early stages of feeling better

5 Recovery + at least 4 months
   Limbic system healed
   Antidepressant no longer needed

**Figure 7 Keeping antidepressants going for long enough –
a schematic representation**

it stops hurting so much. But this doesn't mean that the bone has healed; that takes a few weeks. If, as soon as the pain goes, you take off the plaster and start walking on the recently broken leg, it will re-break.

It's the same with the limbic system. The symptoms of clinical depression start to fade as soon as the levels of the transmitters get back to normal, the nerves return to normal sensitivity and the circuit starts running again. But this doesn't mean it has healed. That takes weeks to months. During this time the antidepressant is propping up the levels of the chemicals. Once the limbic system heals, however, the transmitter levels will stay up of their own accord and you can safely withdraw the medication without feeling any the worse without it.

How long it takes for this healing to take place varies from person to person, but the longer you remain well, the safer you are when you stop taking the drug. We usually advise continuing the antidepressant for **at least six months from the point when you start feeling well**. If you stop it as soon as you feel well, you've got roughly a 60 per cent chance of relapse in the following few weeks. Poor odds. Another month and the risk is in the region of 35 per cent, at three months 20–25 per cent; still too high. At six months it is around 15 per cent, at a year 10 per cent

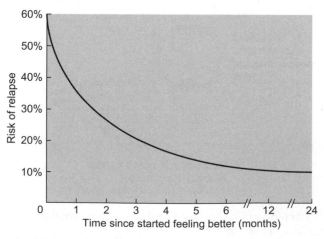

Figure 8 Risk of relapse reduces with longer duration of treatment

and at two years still 10 per cent. We tend to feel that an extra six months of medication for just 5 per cent of extra safety isn't really worth it, hence the advice. Remember, though, the clock doesn't even start until you start feeling well. And if you've had one or more episodes of depressive illness before, healing takes longer, so you'll need to stay on the medication for a year or so. Your doctor will advise you on this.

Try to take your medication regularly. There is a suspicion among experts (though the evidence is as yet sketchy) that taking anti-depressants irregularly may be like taking antibiotics irregularly. Not only may they not work, but you may become permanently resistant to them.

Don't drink a lot of alcohol when you are taking antidepressants. The effect of alcohol can be very unpredictable in the presence of antidepressants; reckon on a drink having anything up to three times its normal effect. What isn't so clear is whether alcohol can interfere with the absorption of these drugs into the body. Better safe than sorry. Keep your drinking to a very moderate level. One drink once or twice a week probably won't do any harm, so long as you don't drive afterwards, but more is a bad idea.

Also, please remember, **don't stop your medication abruptly**. Antidepressants aren't addictive in the full sense of the word, as they don't lose their effect over time, don't require escalating doses to maintain their effect and don't cause craving. But they do potentially have withdrawal symptoms if you stop them suddenly. So don't. Withdraw them over several weeks under the direction of your doctor.

Here are the main classes of antidepressants. Please note that I am not seeking to be comprehensive in my descriptions of their effects and side effects. For a more thorough list I would refer you to *The British National Formulary*, but to be honest, I wouldn't bother. Most of the side effects listed are no more likely to happen to you than a knighthood and studying the list is likely to worry you unneces-sarily. But if you feel I'm patronizing you, go ahead and look your pills up, or question your GP about them. This list includes some general principles and things that are worth looking out for.

Tricyclics

These were the first antidepressants to be used, back in the 1950s. They worked and are still used today. Indeed, at high enough doses, they are at least as effective as any of the modern drugs. One problem, though, is that at these doses they can have quite a few side effects. Most of them are sedative, which is not good if, once you are well, you need to return to work. And you shouldn't drive if you are drowsy, or in any other way impaired. Tricky if you have kids who need driving to school. They mostly have the capacity to cause weight gain. Not everyone suffers this, but occasionally patients can put on a lot of weight. The cause of the problem isn't completely clear, but it is probably mainly due to carbohydrate craving.

The biggest problem with these drugs is that they are exceptionally dangerous in overdosage. Sadly this is something which sometimes happens in people who are severely ill with clinical depression. I'm not desperately keen on these drugs as I don't think that giving a loaded gun to someone who might just use it is a great idea.

Having said that, I do sometimes use tricyclics, as they often work in the minority of cases when the modern drugs fail.

If you do take a tricyclic antidepressant, please take it at the dosage prescribed; they don't work if you take them at too low a dose, or erratically.

Below are listed some of the tricyclics and related drugs (I have extended the category a little), with their particular differences from the others:

Chemical name	Trade name	Differences
amitriptyline	Tryptizol, Lentizol	More sedative.
imipramine	Tofranil	Less sedative.
dosulepin	Prothiaden	Strongly sedative.
doxepin	Sinequan	Zzzzzz! But fewer other side effects.
clomipramine	Anafranil	Sometimes works when other tricyclics don't; also used in obsessional states.
lofepramine	Gamanil	Sometimes fewer side effects.

Monoamine Oxidase Inhibitors (MAOIs)

These drugs, or at least the original ones, aren't often used nowa-days. They are rather inconvenient to take owing to the extensive food restrictions. These include cheese, yeast products (including beer), red wine (particularly Chianti), and any meat which isn't fresh. You're safer avoiding any cooking which has ingredients which aren't known to you, so I'm afraid the Indian takeaway is probably out. You have to take these restrictions seriously; ignoring them could, at worst, lead to a stroke. There are quite a few interac-tions with other medicines too. You need to tell your pharmacist that you're on them before you take any over-the-counter medi-cines. The other problem is that you have to wait a week after you stop most other antidepressants (there are exceptions) before you start an MAOI. If it doesn't work, you then have to wait two weeks before you start anything else.

We still sometimes use these drugs because they quite often work when nothing else does, especially in people who have other psy-chological symptoms on top of their clinical depression.

The newer drug, moclobemide, has many advantages over the older compounds, such as not having to wait the two weeks after stopping it before starting anything else, and being less dangerous if the food restrictions are broken. Unfortunately, it's not clear whether it has the same efficacy in treatment-resistant cases as its older cousins.

Chemical name	Trade name	Differences
phenelzine	Nardil	Slightly sedative.
tranylcypromine	Parnate	Stimulant.
moclobemide	Manerix	Safer, no 'wash-out' period necessary. Same therapeutic profile?

Selective Serotonin Reuptake Inhibitors (SSRIs)

These drugs were a major advance when they came out a decade or so ago, as they were a lot safer and easier to take. So much so that you are put straight on to a dose which is effective for most people, unlike the older drugs, which had to have their doses cranked up slowly to avoid excessive side effects. The first of these compounds to come out is still the most widely prescribed antidepressant in the world, by some distance: Prozac. As their group name suggests, these drugs work on just one of the two chemical systems involved in clinical depression, *serotonin*.

The SSRIs aren't without their problems, but these mostly occur in the first couple of weeks of treatment. Quite a few people suffer some nausea and/or headache during this period, but it is usually manageable and transient. There are anti-nausea drugs and pain-killers available in any case if needed to begin with. A small number of patients, maybe 10 per cent, suffer distressing agitation, though this also doesn't last; in my experience most patients who suffer it tend to bin their tablets as you really don't need more anxiety when you're feeling grim enough anyway. In fact, though, the National Institute of Health and Clinical Excellence (NICE) – a government-appointed quango for which I don't have much time – has taken this side effect very seriously indeed and has advised against the use of SSRIs in adolescents, warning of the potential for an increase in suicide risk and violence in the early stages of taking the drug. Of course, if you experience very severe agitation early on in treat-ment, this could put you at increased risk, and if necessary you may need to stop taking the drug and consult your doctor. However, if these warnings lead to people who suffer only mild side effects early on in the treatment giving up altogether they will have done a grave disservice to people with depressive illness. Most people get nothing very much at all in the way of adverse side effects from SSRIs.

Except, that is, sexual dysfunction. At least 50 per cent of my patients get this to a greater or lesser degree and it may last for as long as you take the tablets (plus a short period while the drug gets out of your system). It's not you, it's the tablets, and some other antidepressants can do the same thing. You may find your sex drive is reduced a bit, but this will usually be more than accounted for by the improvement in libido that results from recovery from the illness. The main problem is delay in reaching orgasm. While this can sometimes be a boon (SSRIs can be used to treat premature ejac-ulation), it doesn't usually work that way. Taking an age to reach climax can, after the novelty has worn off, be pretty harrowing for both of you.

There is no way of telling whether you will get this effect, or whether it will be transient or persist for the duration of treatment. Recently I wished that I possessed a portable trap door to fall through at will. Explaining the unpredictability of this side effect to a patient's wife, I innocently advised: 'You'll just have to suck it and see.' I'll remember the next three seconds of silence for as long as I live. Freud and his slips have a lot to answer for.

Chemical name	Trade name	Differences
fluoxetine	Prozac	Usually ever so slightly stimulant and decreases appetite.
paroxetine	Seroxat	Slightly sedative; useful in depression with anxiety or phobias.
sertraline	Lustral	Usually slightly stimulant.
citalopram	Cipramil	Neither sedative nor stimulant. Lesser incidence of side effects?
fluvoxamine	Faverin	Fewer sexual side effects? More nausea than other SSRIs?
escitalopram	Cipralex	New drug related to citalopram, but may be more potent and with fewer side effects (time will tell).

Other new generation antidepressants

Since the advent of the SSRIs, there have been a number of further drugs becoming available. These reflect the fact that some people don't recover with a drug working on the serotonin system alone. While the other transmitter chemical, *noradrenaline*, usually rises automatically when the levels of serotonin come back to normal, this doesn't always occur. Sometimes the noradrenaline system needs to be tweaked more directly. There was a need for compounds acting, like the tricyclics, on both chemical systems, or specifically noradrenaline, but with fewer side effects and less danger in overdosage. These drugs fit the bill.

Chemical name	Trade name	Differences
venlafaxine	Efexor	Works on both systems. Quite potent. Sometimes weight gain and sex problems. May be less safe in people with heart problems. Occasional blood pressure checks advisable.
mirtazapine	Zispin	Sex problems rare. Powerful sedative. Weight gain sometimes marked. Works on both systems.
reboxetine	Edronax	Slightly stimulant. Works powerfully on noradrenaline only.
duloxetine	Cymbalta	Works on both chemical systems. May not be as potent as venlafaxine, but may be safer in those with heart problems.
agomelatine	Valdoxan	New drug. Works on melatonin system. Mildly sedative. Time will tell on efficacy.
bupropion	Zyban	Works mainly on dopamine, another chemical system not previously thought to be involved in depression. Widely used in the USA, but doesn't have an official licence for use in depression in the UK yet.

Antipsychotic drugs

Just a word about one of these drugs, flupentixol (see list below). Like many things in psychiatry, this was discovered by chance. At many times the strength of the dose used for clinical depression, it is a powerful tranquillizer, used to settle people suffering from psychotic illnesses. At full dosage it does this very well, but researchers found that when the dose goes below about 3mg a day, a switch occurs. Instead of the psychotic patients settling down, they were rushing around in a state of elation. This was obviously hopeless, but sensibly the researchers posed the question whether the drug would also lift the mood of depressed patients. They tried it and it didn't work very well for severely ill depressed patients. But for those with milder clinical depression, and, mixed with another antidepressant for those with more severe depression resistant to the main drug alone, it worked in a good proportion of cases. Because it is used in very small doses (0.5–3mg daily), it usually has no significant side effects. I often find it quite useful.

Other antipsychotic drugs at low dosage also seem to have an antidepressant effect. This may in part be because they can reduce anxiety, so allowing the limbic system to heal. It is also possible that they act on parts of the nerves involved in depression, or even maybe switch off negative feedback loops in these nerve pathways, allowing other antidepressants to act more powerfully. They tend to be used in more treatment-resistant cases of depression, in combination with other antidepressant drugs. Other than flupentixol, they don't yet have a licence to be marketed for treatment of depression, so evidence of efficacy and experience with them is limited.

Chemical name	Trade name	Differences
flupentixol	Fluanxol	Uncertain mode of action. Usually used as 'booster' or for mild depression.
olanzapine	Zyprexa	May cause weight gain. Avoid if diabetic. Like other drugs of this class, caution in people with heart disease.
quetiapine	Seroquel	Can be significantly sedative in some people.
aripiprazole	Abilify	Efficacy not yet certain in depression.

Mood stabilizers

These are drugs normally only used for people who are prone to recurrent episodes of depression which carry on happening despite all other therapeutic efforts, and for people with manic depressive illness (bipolar affective disorder). I'm not dealing with these disorders in this book. But mood stabilizers are also sometimes used in people who are unlucky enough not to respond to antidepressants alone. Also, some people get recurrent episodes of stress-induced depression, which is what this book is about, because the stresses which made them ill in the first place are constant and unavoidable, or recurrent. This is pretty unusual in my experience; as I've already written, there are usually choices available which will allow you to remain well. Mood stabilizers are only, in my view, necessary in recurrent stress-induced depressive illness if every possible stone has been turned in the search for a better way of running your life, without success.

Having said this, they often work. They have changed the lives of people suffering from manic depressive illness for years and more recently they have been found to prevent recurrent depression too, in many cases. The problem isn't their efficacy. But taking any preventative drug poses a problem. What if you remain well for two years, what then? Have you remained well because of the drug, or would you have stayed well anyway? There's no way of telling, other than stopping the drug and seeing what happens. It's impossible to advise when to take this risk; it's a matter of personal choice.

The first mood stabilizer to be discovered, lithium carbonate, is a naturally occurring salt. It's the most frequently effective, though just how effective in stress-induced depression isn't clear yet. We don't know for certain how often it allows recovery to occur when this hasn't been achieved by antidepressants (with or without psychotherapy) alone, but it sometimes does.

I won't go into lithium treatment in detail here; suffice it to say that it is inconvenient to take, mainly because it requires regular blood tests. Without these, there would be a small, but significant, risk to your kidneys. You can't risk your kidneys, because, unlike most other organs in the body, they don't regenerate. So long as you have your blood taken regularly (every 3–6 months – more often to begin with), they are safe. Lithium also occasionally affects the thyroid gland. This isn't a disaster, because thyroid hormone can be replaced in tablet form, and in any case this problem is rare with regular blood monitoring.

You can see why we don't use lithium unless we have to. But for a few people it is a life-saver, as important as insulin to a diabetic.

The other mood stabilizers require less frequent monitoring, but have a rather lower success rate. They are drugs primarily used to control epilepsy, again discovered by chance observation in people suffering from recurrent depressive illness and epilepsy, who were on them for control of the latter, but who then stopped having episodes of the former. Valproate doesn't yet have a licence for use in recurrent depression, but is sometimes used nonetheless.

Chemical name	Trade name	Differences
lithium carbonate	Priadel, Camcolit	Most commonly effective. Blood tests.
valproate	Depakote	Less frequent blood tests required.
carbamazepine	Tegretol	Very occasional blood tests. Slightly sedative.
lamotrigine	Lamictal	Only recently used as a mood stabiliser. Liver function and blood count tests required from time to time.

The rumour in academic circles is that in a few years' time we may have available a test that can tell us who will respond to which drug. This, if it happens, will be an enormous advance. Until then, there is a bit of trial and error in finding the right drug for you. If you're lucky, the first drug you're prescribed will suit you. If not, you may have to try one or two more before you find the right one. Be patient and persevere with the advice of your doctor.

Herbal preparations

I'm not going to go into these in detail here; I believe the rationale for preferring them to be bogus, as I explained earlier. I don't have any objection to using the excreta of the Atlas beetle larva if it has been proven to work better than existing compounds, or have fewer

side effects. But in my experience, the preference for herbal prepara-
tions is usually based on the prejudice that anything made by man
is bad, and by nature, good. Come on, get a critical sense; why are
you following the popular myth?

OK, rant over. St John's Wort is effective in some cases. Many
people seem to tolerate it well, but it probably isn't as good in
severe clinical depression as the medicines listed above. It does have
some interactions with other drugs. Yes, it is a drug. It works on
the same chemical systems as other antidepressants. It isn't on our
prescribing list in the UK at the time of writing, as our Committee
on Safety of Medicines isn't yet satisfied that it is good enough, in
terms of safety or efficacy, to be included. But my guess is that it
probably will be, once some more time and research has passed.

There isn't sufficient evidence available on any other herbal
preparation advertised as treating depression for me to give it to my
dog, let alone recommend it to you, my reader.

Electroconvulsive therapy (ECT)

Having stirred you up about herbal medicine, I don't think this
topic is going to settle you down. It is amazing, the strength of
emotions that this treatment evokes. I get fliers from time to time
from pressure groups quoting selectively from the research on ECT
to try to persuade me never to use it. If you read this stuff, ECT is a
torture. I may be a bit over-imaginative, but it conjures up for me
a Gothic novel.

> 'Igor, bring me the electrodes, the victi—. . . the patient is ready.'
> 'Yehths, Mahthter, then shall I prepare the virgins?'
> 'You know what to do, Igor. We must be ready when the
> Master of Evil arrives.'

Oh, give me a break, will you, do I look stupid? I can't be
doing with zealots. Anyone can make a point by emphasizing one
research finding while ignoring another. No, let's look at ECT dis-
passionately, not as a matter of religious faith.

ECT involves passing a small electrical current between the two
sides of the head of an anaesthetized patient, twice a week, usually
for two to four weeks (four to eight treatments). In severe clinical

depression it has the highest success rate, in the quickest time, of any available treatment. However, this is clearly not a treatment to be undertaken lightly. While the anaesthetic is only about 5 minutes long, having two anaesthetics a week is no joke.

The most important common problem is memory disturbance. Not everyone gets this, especially nowadays, as only a small fraction of the amount of electricity is delivered as used to be the case in the old days. But if you do, it can be a major issue. Most of the research on this suggests that the problem is a temporary one. It seems that during the course of ECT, many patients suffer pretty hazy memory. You may forget the names of people you know well, your daughter's address, or other well-known details. Once the course of ECT is completed, the memory disturbance shrinks. That is, you can remember things you learnt well before the ECT started, but not necessarily things that happened in the period just before the treatments started or during the course of them. This 'island' of lost memories continues to shrink until, after between a few weeks and, at most, a year, the only period for which you still have no memory is the period during which you had the ECT treatments. You may feel that this period isn't much of a loss.

While this is what the research suggests, a few patients are very clear that ECT has permanently harmed their ability to remember new information, or even to think with their previous clarity. It's difficult to explain this discrepancy. Maybe this is another example of research failing to pick up unusual events, or maybe it is a case of retrospect giving an exaggerated impression of your past mental prowess. I don't know. I can't guarantee that you will suffer no permanent harm to your memory from ECT, but it's very unlikely. (If you want to know more about this treatment, try the Royal College of Psychiatrists website, <http://www.rcpsych.org.uk> and follow the links to their information sheet on ECT.)

Most psychiatrists still use ECT, but only rarely, *in extremis*. I only suggest it if my patient is at risk of serious harm because he has stopped eating and/or drinking, if all other available treatments have failed (it takes a long time to try them all), or if, subjectively, the torment of his illness is so dreadful that a compassionate human being cannot leave him in his hell-hole for a day longer than necessary. In these cases, it can be a life-saver. And, if you talk to people who have had it, it isn't a distressing experience, any more than any anaesthetic is.

The future

There are a number of new antidepressant drugs being trialled as we speak. Among other lines of enquiry, researchers are looking at whether drugs working on hormonal systems may be effective. Maybe drugs working on the cortisol system (see earlier) may have an antidepressant effect? We already know that some women with depression respond to hormonal treatments and that thyroid hormones occasionally help people with resistant depression.

The 'new ECT' is a technique called 'deep brain stimulation' (DBS), which involves placing a device in the skull that passes electrical pulses through electrodes to certain parts of the brain, such as the frontal cortex. Early research is promising, but it is very early days as yet, and if it ever takes off it would only be used, like ECT, for people who are dangerously ill and have not responded to less invasive treatments. Don't expect your doctor to recommend DBS any time soon.

This list of treatments isn't comprehensive, but it includes most of the questions I'm most commonly asked and the misconceptions with which I'm most commonly confronted. If in doubt, ask your doctor, not your neighbour, especially if she's got strong opinions. People with the strongest opinions are often those with the least knowledge as, once you consider any issue seriously, you will often find that it defies a categorical opinion one way or the other.

9

More about treatments – psychotherapies

If you can answer the three questions I posed in Chapter 7, and if you can change the way you run your life based on these answers, you don't need psychotherapy. You can probably look forward to a happier and healthier life. You will look back on this episode of depressive illness as a blessing, the pivotal point when your life turned around for the better. But it may not be as easy as that. You may find yourself compelled to keep overloading, neglecting and abusing yourself for reasons you can't fathom. Then you need psychotherapy of one kind or another.

More has been written about psychotherapy than about the rest of psychiatry put together. I'm not a psychotherapist, just a jobbing psychiatrist, so I won't attempt to explain the intricacies of the art here, but some basic principles may be helpful for you to understand what you are going to be doing and why.

Counselling and short-term focal psychotherapy

As I explained earlier, under the NHS you are more likely to be offered straightforward counselling than full-blown psychotherapy. A counsellor does what a friend would do if she were sufficiently well informed, lacking in preconceptions and patient. Friends have a tendency to give you advice. This is based on *their* experiences and circumstances, not yours. Anyone who has been through a divorce will know how many friends need you to act out their anger towards your departing spouse, and how unhelpful is their counsel. When you don't take their advice, they then tend to take their anger out on you. If you keep going over the same ground, without *doing* anything, they tend to lose interest and stop calling you. So you stop talking about your problems and feelings and just put on a brave face.

But often what you really need is to go over the same feelings again and again, *without doing anything*. If you don't know which way to go, stay still until the way becomes clear. A counsellor will help you to do this, facing your feelings and issues face on, and in due course making the changes you need, but not reacting impulsively in ways which will only make things worse.

In short-term focal psychotherapy you will go a bit deeper than this. While your therapist will make no deliberate effort to work with you on issues and events from your past, you have probably been acting in the ways which eventually made you ill, all your life. There are reasons for this. We learn how to feel early on in our lives and as often as not our actions at times when things are tough reflect those feelings. Neglectful parents teach their kids that they aren't worth much. Ironically, when those children grow up they tend to lavish enormous love and care on their undeserving mother and father, in a hopeless attempt at gaining the love and approval they crave (see Chapter 3). When things go wrong in their lives, they give out even more. The fuse blows. For this pattern to change, your psychotherapist has to help you to accept that it isn't going to happen. You'll never get their love, not properly, as they don't know how to give it. In the field of love-giving, they are disabled. You need to accept their disability and learn how to get love from others, including yourself, and notice when it is being given to you. Your therapist will help you with this, mostly focussing on here-and-now issues, rather than on the distant past. There are many variations on this theme, but the principles are the same. Face and accept the realities of your life and then make the decisions and take the opportunities that present themselves. This is what focal psychotherapy is about.

Individual psychodynamic psychotherapy

Sometimes the problems are more complex, without a clear focus to the issue. In any case, your needs may be conflicting. This type of stress, when your different needs are in opposite directions, is particularly liable to make you ill. For example, you may need to earn more money, but also spend more time with your wife and kids. You may need the love and approval of your father, but also to give him a piece of your mind. These *conflicts* need to be resolved, to avoid you spending your life racing around in ever-decreasing circles. In these cases, it may be necessary to make a wider-ranging exploration of your whole life. Psychodynamic psychotherapy seeks to identify the driving (or psychodynamic) issues in your life. However, this aspect, the gaining of insight into the roots of one's problems, is only a small part of the therapy. Some people expect the therapist to listen for a while, then to exclaim in a German accent, 'You ver clearly bitten by ze dog ven you ver a leetle beby, leading to ghre-pressed Oedipal oourges undt latent homoerotic fantazies!'

"There's nothing I can do for you – you are a duck."

© *Punch Ltd*

It doesn't work like that. Identifying the root of your problems does not make them go away. Insight doesn't lead automatically to cure. However, it does give you something to work on, hence the need to explore your past. Having found those issues throughout your life that you didn't deal with at the time, you need now to *work them through*. This process is easiest to understand with reference to a phenomenon that I'm specifically not dealing with in this book: grieving. Most people know that, if you lose a loved one, you have to grieve. If you don't do so at the time, the grief will drip away through your life in the decades that follow. Grieving, painful though it is, allows you, in due course, to move on. It isn't ever OK; of course it isn't. But you are able to be *free*. Free to experience the whole range of human emotions, rather than just sadness. To be sad sometimes, desolate occasionally, and at other times, unexpectedly, to experience pleasure, and even joy. If you are experiencing grief right now, you won't believe this to be possible; the mere sugges-tion is probably slightly offensive. But feel, without pushing your feelings away, and, mark my words, it will happen.

This is working through; the working through of a terrible loss.

The process of psychotherapy does the same thing. You are being taken through a grieving process, in a way, for what should have been. In the same way that someone emerges from grief if he faces it, you emerge from psychotherapy more healthy by working through those issues that you didn't deal with at the time.

In psychodynamic psychotherapy there is a powerful tool available to accelerate this process, which happens automatically. It is called *transference*. If a therapist stays still enough and resists the urge to give advice, but just stays with the feelings being presented, over time her client will develop powerful feelings towards her. These feelings will tend to mirror feelings he has experienced before, towards central figures in his life. This time he can work them through. As a child he could not be angry with the mother who was punishing and neglecting him; to do so would only have attracted further punishment. Now he can experience anger towards his therapist, even maybe express it. No disaster occurs, but he is given the opportunity to work it through. Thus he gains a more accurate perspective; he doesn't turn the anger against himself; he understands his mother for who she was; he stops trying to please her (after all she has been dead since 1977), and he lets himself be.

If this sounds simple, it isn't. Psychotherapy is stressful. It is a powerful drug and, like all drugs, it has side effects. It seeks to awaken emotions in order to work them through, not to pour oil on the waters. It isn't for the faint-hearted; indeed, fragile people who have scant personal resources don't do well in psychotherapy, but fortunately they are rare among sufferers from clinical depression anyway. More seriously, someone who has been keeping a precarious balance in her life through the defences she has developed, may become seriously compromised should those defences be challenged inappropriately by an inexperienced or poorly trained therapist. Such therapists do exist. I've seen them blunder through the delicate balance of damaged but courageous patients' lives, leaving carnage in the wake of their good intentions. Avoid therapists who want to help you too much. Take a recommendation from someone in the field. In my experience, good psychotherapists cannot be manufactured, so qualifications are no guarantee. No, ask one of my colleagues, or your GP; they'll direct you to a good one.

Your role in therapy is equally important. In my view the single most important determinant in the success or failure of psycho-therapy is the degree of *acting out*. This refers to *acting* on your feelings and emotions *outside* the therapy sessions. The opposite is *talking* or *working in therapy*. If you act out your issues, nothing ever changes because there is no emotion left for the work of therapy. And it is emotion that is the fuel of therapy.

Let's assume you have difficulties with angry feelings, which you sometimes direct towards others, with harmful results on your relationships, and sometimes turn against yourself. You are referred to a psychotherapist. On the way to your weekly session you meet the usual idiotic behaviour of your fellow motorists. You could lapse into road rage, shouting, waving your fist, making gestures implying they have solitary sex lives, and driving six inches from the bumper of the car in front of you. By the time you get to the session, you'll feel a bit better, because you've discharged your anger by acting it out. There won't be any anger left to take into the session, which will get nowhere, becoming a detached the-oretical exercise. Psychotherapy needs real, here-and-now emotion. Alternatively, you could resist the urge to road rage, storing up your frustrations for the session. In the hands of a skilled therapist it won't take long to divert your anger from motorists to the people who really earned it, be they mother, father, teacher, spouse or whoever. Then you can start working it through and as a result, in due course, free yourself from its shackles.

The commonest form of acting out that I see in my patients is excessive caring. There are times when, as I tell my patient to forge more time and space for herself, I know she won't do so; I can see it in her eyes. She is spending her life running away from guilt, having traded her guilt for a lorry-load of exhaustion and quiet, resigned resentment. Therapy doesn't work, because she is too busy rushing around tending to folks for it to take hold. Soon enough she drops therapy as she hasn't got time for it.

If she's you, then I'm sorry, but you're choosing illness. Recognize what you're doing and take responsibility for it. When you're ready, make a different choice. Feel guilty, not resentful, exhausted and ill. Your guilt won't harm you. Indeed, it is grist to the therapeutic mill, if you'll only let it happen and take it into the sessions.

Finally, how long does psychodynamic psychotherapy take? I

don't know; it varies from a few months to several years. But if you're embarked on a course of this type of therapy, I've got a rule of thumb. This was given to me by my first psychotherapy teacher. It's the rule of thirds; it has proven remarkably accurate in my experience since. This rule states that psychotherapy is divided into three periods, which turn out to be of roughly equal length.

The first third is *beginning*. This is the phase of getting into the therapy, identifying and overcoming the resistances and gaining sufficient trust to get past the superficial. The second third is the *work* of therapy. This is when things really happen which allow enduring change to occur. The last third is *ending*. This phase needs quite a bit of working through, because if you've been using your therapist properly, you will have developed a degree of dependence on her. You don't have to avoid or be frightened of developing dependence on your therapist; it is a good sign, but it has to be carefully managed during the therapy, and worked through during the process of ending, in order to let you move on with your life, looking forward rather than back.

So, if you're just beginning to get into the therapy and things are happening at last, it's a fair bet that you've got about twice as long to go as you've already done.

One more thing. I mentioned this in Chapter 3 but it bears repeating. Don't be misled by my style – I like answers and have some pretty clear thoughts on this illness, but psychodynamic psychotherapy is an unstructured process. You won't find an instruction manual to tell you what to do; it's an exploration in which you, not your therapist, decide on the direction and the answers.

Cognitive behavioural therapy (CBT)

Cognitive behavioural therapy, in the hands of a skilled therapist, is beautifully simple. It simply invites you to look at the truth accurately, rather than in your usual selectively negative fashion. This can usually be achieved reasonably quickly, compared with the time it takes to achieve results with exploratory psychotherapy. However, this depends on the amount of time and effort you are prepared to devote to it. Cognitive behavioural therapy usually involves a considerable amount of homework and its success depends on you doing the work properly. While you would have thought that the sort of people who get clinical depression would be sure to pursue this task with diligence, this isn't always the case: they seem often to have a blind spot for doing the work necessary to stay well.

There are several reasons for this. First, the treatment is often started too soon. In the pits of depression, you can't make a cup of tea, let alone keep a complex diary of thoughts and alternative self-statements. In my view, cognitive behavioural therapy is, in any case, better at *keeping* you well than *getting* you well, so there's no enormous hurry to get it started. There is always a bit of a conflict between the needs for rest in early recovery and the needs of the therapy for homework. You'll just have to make your own judgements on this as you go along. Concentrate more on resting early on, but more on the therapy once you are quite a bit better.

Second, you tend to think of yourself as bottom of the list of priorities. By the time you have kept everyone else happy, you've already overdone it and so have no time or energy left for working at the therapy. Third, there is a part of you which is self-destructive (see 'Overactive superego', 'Anger turned inward', Chapter 3). This part will tend to have you subconsciously sabotaging the treatment, by passively resisting the therapist's efforts. I can testify how frustrating this is for the psychiatrist, let alone the therapist, but of course if I give vent to this frustration, it just confirms my patient's preconception that he will always fail and be a disappointment, so I try not to. What I do is to point out what is going on. If your actions are made conscious, you have real choice. You could choose to overrule your self-destructive tendency and, against your instincts, do the work you need to do.

Finally, the exact same thought patterns that underpin depression (see 'Learned helplessness', Chapter 3, and 'Cognitive theory', Chapter 4) and are symptoms of the illness will tend to dissuade you from working on yourself and your needs. 'Oh, what's the point, it won't work; nothing ever does; in any case, I can't do anything about my life.'

Look, forget your judgements about whether or not things will change. It doesn't matter much whether or not you believe in the therapy, whether you enjoy it, or whether you want to do it. *Just do it*. The point of it will emerge later.

If you do the work in between the sessions that your therapist asks of you, there is an excellent chance of success. Cognitive behavioural therapy has a proven track record. From my observation, there is a fair chance of achieving the changes that you need to in between six and twenty sessions. If your sessions are weekly, that probably means between six weeks and six months of therapy. After that, it's down to you. Cognitive behavioural therapy only works if your changed way of thinking leads to a change in the way you operate. However accurately you see yourself, the world and the future, if you again put 18 amps through a 13-amp fuse, it will again blow.

Cognitive behavioural therapy comes in several variations. Recently a form has developed that incorporates elements of exploratory psychotherapy with cognitive principles. It is called cognitive analytical therapy (CAT). However, there are more similarities than differences in these variants. Whichever type you have, you are likely to be asked to keep a diary. Whenever you feel particularly bad, you will be expected to record what has happened and the thoughts that the events generated in you. After a few sessions a pattern of a characteristic type of self-defeating and inaccurate thinking is likely to emerge. Your therapist will then start to help you to challenge these thoughts and the deeply held underlying assumptions that generate them. In your homework, you will go beyond just recording your negative thoughts, to generating some alternative explanations and even rating the likelihood of each being correct. At the next session your therapist will go through these thoughts, the alternatives and their relative likelihoods with you, helping you to challenge your thoughts' validity.

For example, take the man in the cartoon in Chapter 4 who assumes he is going to be sacked because his boss ignores him in the corridor. The entry in his diary might look like this:

Date:

Event	Thought	Mood 0 = Worst 10 = Best	Alternatives	%
Boss ignored me in the corridor.	He is angry with me.	1	He is angry with me.	50%
			He was thinking of something else and didn't see me.	25%
			He was looking at his watch and didn't see me.	25%

Your therapist will go through this entry with you, looking at your assumptions, identifying your catastrophic line of thinking (which ends with the debtors' prison for you and starvation for your family), challenging it, helping you to generate other possible interpretations for the event and then enabling you to alter the percentage likelihood of each conclusion. In due course other columns may be added to your diary, such as one for the basic assumption underlying the thought (e.g. I'm no good), and a revised mood score, having gone through the process of generating alternative, less catastrophic conclusions.

Over a period of time you will notice an increasing gap between the initial very low mood which follows the negative thought and the better mood which follows your re-analysis of your conclusions. You are gaining control of your thoughts. Eventually your underlying assumptions will shift too and there will be fewer events and negative thoughts to report. Now use your more accurate thinking to make some choices in your life. The disaster that you always assumed would follow doing what you want and making a shift in your own favour, probably won't. You're now beginning to realize that and to see the exciting possibilities that it brings. Grab the opportunity. Some people will be unhappy about these changes, though not your real friends. In any case, it is their responsibility to adapt to the new order of things, not yours to organize it for them. This isn't belligerence, it is common sense. You can't change the fact that, if you are going to do more for yourself, you will be doing less for some others. Those who have got used to using your goodwill will take some time to adapt and won't always like it however you dress it up. Understand their discomfort sympathetically, but stick to your guns.

It's worth checking, from time to time, that you aren't slipping back into old ways. You can do this by noting the language you use. If you frequently use the words in the left-hand column overleaf, you need to do some more work on your thinking. If those in the right-hand column turn up more often, you'll probably achieve health and happiness.

Illness words	Wellness words
Must	Want
Have to	Choose
Fail	Learn
100%	Balance
Can't	Can
Resentment	Responsibility
What if	Opportunity

Mindfulness (-based CBT)

I outlined the rational basis of the mindfulness approach on page 37. Some people struggle with the structured, logic-based approach of CBT. Mindfulness, or mindfulness-based CBT (MBCBT), is an offshoot of CBT, and borrows from concepts developed in eastern philosophies and religions such as Buddhism, which can suit these folk better. Among its principles are learning to stay in the present moment, rather than ruminating about the past and future, and experiencing rather than doing battle with feelings, emotions, symptoms, circumstances and events. So if you are feeling panicky about something that you fear may happen, your therapist will teach you to focus on what is going on now, to observe your panicky symptoms, how they build, plateau and then fade. Don't try to make them go away; they will do that of their own accord once you stop grappling with them. It isn't your panic, or fear, that is the problem, it is your *fear of fear*. Step back and watch it, and it will fade.

MBCBT has an increasingly strong evidence base.

Ways of thinking

So how should you think, having dismantled your old way of viewing the world? Within the limits of a short chapter in a short book it is difficult to answer this fundamental question; there are so many different ways of looking at it. However, the first recorded cognitive behavioural therapist had some pretty good answers; you could do worse than view the world the way he did.

Epictetus* was a slave living in what is now Turkey, then under Roman control. Much of the time he was chained to a stake by a leg shackle which, on one occasion, his master wished to tighten, lest he should escape. Epictetus argued that this should not be done, pointing out that there was no way for him to escape anyway and that the only end tightening the shackle would achieve would be the breaking of his leg. His master, not one to be dictated to by a slave, ignored him and tightened the shackle, resulting predictably in the leg being broken.

Epictetus reacted with no sign of distress or complaint. His master was astounded and asked the slave why he had under-reacted so. Epictetus replied that there was no point in complaint, distress or further argument as his leg was already broken and nothing could reverse the fact. This and further demonstrations of rational thinking made a big impression on the Roman, who eventually released him as a free man, with enough money to make his way as a philosopher. This he did to great effect, influencing the writings of a number of the major thinkers of his day. His way of viewing the world has stood the test of time and, in my view, can form the basis of a healthy outlook now.

Epictetus pointed out that it is not events or other people that do us the most harm; it's how we view and react to them. Our choice in the world is not over our circumstances, which are often outside our control, but we can decide upon our reaction to them. Depending upon our choices, we can make serenity out of adversity, or vexation out of privilege. In any case, knowing what is and what isn't under your control is a key to being as effective as possible without getting overheated over things you can't influence (see 'Cognitive dissonance', Chapter 4). Don't demand that the world reacts the way you want it to, or that what you wish for should always happen. This will lead to frustration and disillusionment. The world and other people may work to different rules and needs from yours. Accept this and make the most of what comes to you.

There really is nothing to lose, as it isn't ours anyway. It's only on loan from the world (or God, if you like), including life itself. You haven't lost it; it has merely been returned whence it came. Take

---

* with thanks to John Winston Bush, *Epictetus: The Fundamentals*

care of what you have while it's there, not as its owner, but as its guardian, as you would a room in a hotel.

We react in certain predictable ways, by habit. How things turn out depends upon what those habits are. They become more ingrained by practice, or can be changed by practising another way of acting. The more often and the more circumstances in which we do something, the more it becomes a habit. So do more of what you want to become and less of what you want to move away from; do something else instead. Or, putting it another way: you become the way that you act (see Chapter 3).

All of these ways of thinking go back two millennia. They work.

Cognitive behavioural therapy is a kind of philosophy, which is itself just a way of accurately viewing the world. No doubt you have your own favourite philosophies and sayings. Use them in your day-to-day life, whether they originate from the Bible or the back of a cornflakes packet. Some of my own include the writings of Max Ehrmann, Richard Bach, Kahlil Gibran, Eckhart Tolle and Neale Donald Walsch (the last of these, from his account writing the words of God) and the reported teachings of Christ. I'm not going to try to do justice to these writings here; better to read them for yourself:

- 'Desiderata' and 'Whatever Else You Do', by Max Ehrmann.
- *Illusions*, *One* and *Jonathan Livingstone Seagull*, by Richard Bach.
- *The Prophet*, by Kahlil Gibran.
- *Conversations with God – Books 1–3*, by Neale Donald Walsch.
- *The Power of Now*, by Eckhart Tolle.
- The words of Christ in the Holy Bible.

Well, all right then, just a couple of quotes to whet your appetite:

'Here is a test to find whether your mission on earth is finished: if you're alive, it isn't' (life is a continuous process of learning, it doesn't stop till you die) – from *Illusions*.

'. . . in the noisy confusion of life, keep peace in your soul. With all its sham, drudgery and broken dreams, it is still a beautiful world. Be cheerful. Strive to be happy' – from 'Desiderata'.

10

Some skills for problem areas

People who get stress-induced depressive illness tend to run too hot. They spend too much of their lives putting in too much effort. When confronted by a sea of troubles, they try to deal with them all at once. By now this will be a familiar picture. When they get overwhelmed they just push harder. Because they are so overaroused, they have difficulty in getting to sleep and then, when they become ill, they start waking in the early hours of the morning as well. Then they deal with the mounting tiredness by trying to push their way through it. So the conditions are in place for the fuse to blow.

Part of the solution, as I have outlined in previous chapters, is to change the way you operate, so you take on less and reserve more time and space for yourself. The other part is to learn some skills that allow you to run at a lower level of arousal in any given situation. This will help you feel less anxious and make it easier to sleep well; there are other ways of sleeping better, too. They don't work once you have developed clinical depression, but they can help to prevent illness occurring in the first place.

What is more, they can prevent you getting hooked on sleeping tablets. These drugs are fine when taken occasionally, but have a tendency, like all addictive drugs, to make things worse in the long run if taken regularly for long periods. They vary in this regard, with drugs like Temazepam having among the greatest capacities for causing problems in long-term usage, while the sedative antihistamines such as Nytol and Phenergan are a lot safer. Best of all, though, don't use any sleeping medication regularly. And above all, *don't use alcohol to help you sleep*. It will make things worse.

Incidentally, if you have read my previous book *Dying for a Drink*, you need go no further with this chapter. The principles of stress management are the same whatever the nature of your affliction.

Relaxation

The best way to combat stress is to learn and become expert at a relaxation exercise. There are many variations on this theme and the thing is to find the one that works best for you. There are several relaxation tapes commercially available and many people find it easiest to learn the techniques by listening to one of these. Others get benefit from yoga techniques learnt in a group setting. Some find that following a written set of instructions helps them better, by allowing them to do the exercise at their own pace with their own mental imagery. What follows is just one example of such a technique, but one which many of my patients have found helpful.

Whichever way you choose, the essential point is that it needs a lot of practice. Though a few people pick it up very quickly, for the majority relaxation exercises do not work at all to begin with. Some people even feel worse at the beginning, because doing anything and having it fail tends to make you feel tense.

Persevere, because when you really master the technique you will find that it changes your life, allowing you to deal with situations that previously you could not have coped with at all. The people who get benefit from relaxation exercises are those who put them top of their list of priorities and practise for at least half an hour every day, come hell or high water.

Looking back, I did relaxation exercises every day for about three years, not because I was unusually anxious but because I thought then, as now, that everybody can benefit from them. It took me about a month of daily practice for the exercise to be any use at all. It took at least three months to get to the stage of being able to use it before an exam, because the most difficult time to do a relaxation exercise effectively is when you most need it, at times of high stress. In about two to three years I got to the stage of no longer needing the exercise because I could switch on the relaxed state like a light when necessary. I can tell you that gaining this ability is worth all the time and effort.

A relaxation exercise

Spend 15–20 minutes on this exercise.

1 Find a suitable place to relax. A bed or an easy chair is ideal, but anywhere will do, preferably quiet and private. If your seat in the office or a house full of children is all there is, it can still be done.
2 Try to clear your mind of thoughts as far as you can.
3 Take three very slow very deep breaths (10–15 seconds to breathe in and out once).
4 Imagine a neutral figure. An example might be the number 1. Don't choose any object or figure with an emotional significance, such as a ring or a person, for example. Let it fill your mind. See it in your mind's eye, give it a colour, try to see it in 3-D and repeat it to yourself, under your breath, many times over. Continue until it fills your mind.
5 Slowly change to imagine yourself in a quiet, peaceful and pleasurable place or situation. This may be a favourite place or situation, or a pleasant scene from your past. Be there, and notice all the feelings, in each sense. See it, feel it, hear it and smell it. Spend some time there.
6 Slowly change to be aware of your body. Notice any tension in your body. Take each group of muscles in turn, and tense, then relax them two or three times each. Include fingers, hands, arms, shoulders, neck, face, chest, tummy, buttocks, thighs, legs, feet

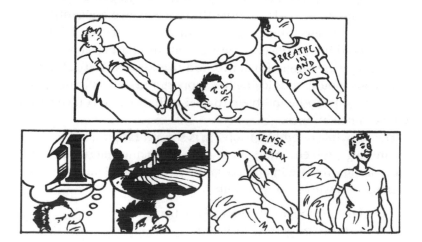

and toes. Be aware of the feeling of relaxation. When complete, spend some time in this relaxed state.

7 Slowly get up and go about your business.

At step 5, I want to emphasize that this isn't simply visualization. It is a *multisensory experience*. Let me demonstrate. You are imagining yourself on a beautiful Caribbean beach. Lovely. But that isn't enough. Which direction is the wind coming from? Is it constant or puffy? What does it feel like when the sun goes behind a cloud? Does it get cooler? What does hot sun on sand smell of and what is the smell of your suntan lotion? Is the sand soft or hard? How do the waves sound? What does your drink taste of? How far back does the grass start? Are the palm trees small stumpy palms or tall coconut palms? If they are coconut palms, are the coconuts brown or green?

You need to be there in every sense. This takes quite a lot of practice.

Don't hurry this procedure and remember to practise. It will work.

Problem-solving

The trouble with problems is that they don't come one at a time but, like buses, in batches. When you are in one of these spells, the weight of problems seems so overwhelming that you don't know where to start. The whole thing seems like a gigantic mess. You can't tolerate things being out of control, so you try to deal with everything at once, resulting only in chasing your tail and becoming increasingly frustrated and overheated. You get irritable with your spouse, thus losing her support and understanding. Now you have yet another problem to deal with, because you've tried to do too much at once.

The principle of problem-solving is simple: take a set of problems or one big problem and split it up into smaller pieces. Let's take an example. You are in a financial mess. This problem is too big to manage as a whole, so split it up:

1 I'm above my overdraft limit at the bank.
2 My creditors are getting insistent.

3 I'm spending beyond my means.
4 My debtors aren't paying up.
5 The mortgage rate has gone up.
6 The car is on its last legs.
7 Christmas is just around the corner.

Now you have a set of smaller and more manageable problems to sort out. Take each one in turn and 'brainstorm' some possible actions. This means including all your ideas on what to do, the apparently bad ones as well as the obviously sensible ones. For example, for Problem 1 a possible list might be:

a Ask the manager to extend my overdraft limit.
b Explain that the problem is largely of cash flow, that I am addressing it and it should only be temporary.
c Take out a short-term loan.
d Borrow from friends/relatives.
e Cut out items of expenditure (see Problem 3).
f Ignore it.
g Do more overtime.
h Move house.
i Change job.

Now think each option through and reject those that don't work. Talk it through with someone, if it helps.

Do this process for each of the points that you originally listed. Several of the action points will recur. Gather them together and then put them in a list of priority and act on them one at a time. Tick them off as you do each one. The process of working through the list is very satisfying and allows you to feel that you are doing everything that can be done to improve the situation.

Of course, following this structure for problems does not make them go away, but it does give you more control over them. Stress tends to happen when you feel that you have lost control over your life. You can't get the control back through effort alone. You need to act strategically, with organization and patience. Don't try to make it all happen at once.

Time management

I tend to rush around at a hundred miles an hour, not always achieving a lot. When it was suggested to me that I was stressing myself unnecessarily and that I needed a time-management programme, I protested: 'It isn't that I don't manage my time, there just isn't enough time to do everything.' However, a kindly person ignored my protestations and designed a time plan for me anyway. This involved organizing my day so that I was doing tasks together that could be done in one place, pulling together blocks of time for paperwork and having slots through the week left empty for emergencies and unforeseen circumstances. As a result, I am getting through a lot more work and am much less stressed. The only bit of it I don't like is being proved wrong.

If you find yourself harassed and overburdened, I would strongly recommend that you draw up a weekly time plan, with spaces

	Monday	Tuesday	Wednesday	Thursday	Friday	Saturday	Sunday
9 a.m.				filing	deliver report	shopping	
10 a.m.	admin meeting	spare for crises and problems	personal work	computer work	travel		
11 a.m.							
Noon				prepare reports	meet with client		
1 p.m.		L	U N	C H			rest
2 p.m.	personal work	travelling	presentation	meeting about report	travel personal work		
3 p.m.		meeting	rest			rest	
4 p.m.			travelling	admin	prepare next week's time plan		
5 p.m.							
Evening	rest	prepare presentation	late meeting	going out	rest	theatre	

for unforeseen events and for rest. This works even for the most irregular of lifestyles, such as bringing up children.

Thought-stopping

When you are stressed you often find that a thought sticks in your mind and you can't get rid of it. If you try to clear it out of your mind it keeps coming back, and mulling it over time and again makes you even more tense. The following technique, again with practice, can help you to clear your mind so that you can get on with what you are doing or think about something else.

When you are alone, suddenly make a loud noise. Remember the sudden sensation.

When you find yourself mulling over repetitive thoughts, bring this memory into your mind. Allow it to give you a jolt.

Say sharply to yourself: 'Stop!' This does not have to be out loud, but imagine yourself saying it sharply and loudly.

Substitute another thought that is relevant and realistic in your situation, or go and do something that requires concentration.

Sleep tips

Depressive illness wrecks your sleep. Usually your sleep pattern will return to normal once recovery has occurred, but sometimes poor sleep, resulting from running too hot, predates the illness. There are ways of sleeping better without sleeping tablets.

Catnaps and siestas

Your sleep requirement is calculated as a total over 24 hours. If you sleep for a couple of hours during the day, the total sleep you can expect the next night will fall by two hours. The loss usually occurs in the first half of the night, so it feels as if you can't get to sleep at the time that you feel you should. In fact, your usual 11 p.m. has just been delayed to around 1 a.m. If you get upset about this, sleep may be delayed further (see below).

The effect of short-term sleep loss

You have got an important meeting tomorrow at which you have to give a difficult presentation. 'I must get a good night's sleep so that I am at my best. I know that so-and-so Wilkins is going to give me a hard time, so I have to be on my toes,' you say to yourself. Instead of your usual midnight bedtime you retire at 9.30 p.m.

The trouble is that you have a biological clock inside you which is set for sleep at around 11 p.m. You lie in bed and concentrate hard on getting to sleep. After ten minutes you are still awake. You redouble your efforts. Your eyes are clamped shut, your jaw juts out, your neck veins protrude and your face contorts into a picture of tense concentration with your efforts at sleep. This is a suitable attitude for a fight to the death with a grizzly bear but not for slumber.

The clock shows 11 p.m. 'Oh no! I'm not going to get any more sleep than usual, I *must* get to sleep.' You are tense and aroused. As midnight passes you begin to get really worried. 'I'm going to be a wreck tomorrow, it will be a disaster.' You toss and turn until the early hours, when eventually fatigue overcomes your state of arousal and you sink into a troubled sleep. You sleep through the alarm and arrive late for the meeting, flustered and weary. Your worst fears are realized and Wilkins has a ball at your expense.

If only you had realized this simple fact: one night's sleep loss isn't a major problem. It wasn't the lost sleep that spoilt your presentation; it was the fact that you spent the night worrying about not sleeping. Worry and tension are very wearing. Adrenaline has been pumping around your body all night, so that at the time you needed it, for the meeting, there was none left and you were exhausted.

There have been lots of studies which have confirmed this. Subjects are deprived of a night's sleep and then tested on a range of mental and manual skills. On most tests there isn't a lot of difference between their performance and that of subjects who have been given a full night's sleep, but because the test results are of no concern to them they haven't worried about their sleep loss.

Of course, if you are deprived of sleep regularly, you do suffer. I remember when I was a houseman (a first-year junior doctor – the dogsbody) once having a particularly busy weekend on call. I didn't get to bed from Friday morning to Monday evening. I was OK for the first part of the weekend, but Sunday night was tough and I am told that on Monday afternoon I arrived for the ward round looking perplexed and asking where I was and why I was here. Fortunately, with the new rules on doctors' hours, this rarely occurs nowadays, but it was an interesting if alarming experience of the effects of repeated sleep deprivation.

Presuming that you are not unfortunate enough to have this kind of job, the best advice is to have a regular time to go to bed and to stick to it. If you can't sleep on one particular night, don't worry. Instead, practise a relaxation exercise (see page 93). Effective relaxation confers many of the restorative benefits of sleep and will allow you to be fighting fit the next day, whether you sleep well or not.

Tea and coffee

Most Britons drink a lot of coffee and/or tea. Both contain caffeine, a stimulant drug with a similar, though much weaker, effect to amphetamine. Another memory of mine is of burning the midnight oil when revising for my final medical exams. I had a filter coffee machine, the type that sits in a glass jug on a hotplate to keep warm. As I worked through the night, I drank my way through several jugs of this brew. What I hadn't realized was that, when left to stand, the water was being lost from the coffee in the jug through heating, so the stuff that I was drinking was super-strength. At about 2 a.m. I started to feel strange. The symptoms were of anxiety, restlessness, slight tremor, palpitations and inability to think straight. When I went to bed I was unable to sleep. I was suffering from caffeine intoxication, and most unpleasant it was too.

It is often the custom to finish an evening meal with strong coffee. Many people have several cups in an evening. This is enough to spoil your sleep. If you have difficulty sleeping, it is wise to have your last cup before 6 p.m. Also, look out for some soft drinks. Many contain caffeine in considerable amounts.

As an aside, I believe that many people are addicted to coffee. Try sometime going a whole working day without a cup. You may well feel tired, lethargic and unable to think with your usual clarity. This is caffeine withdrawal. People who have abandoned coffee and tea or turned to decaffeinated brands often say that they feel a lot better for it.

A hot milky drink

The manufacturers of Horlicks and other such beverages have long extolled their virtues to assist good sleep. Most of us treat this claim sceptically, but in fact it is based on sound scientific fact. The benefits of these drinks can mostly be gained by a cup of hot milk, but Horlicks tastes better.

Milk is rich in protein, carbohydrate and fat. The presence of these foods in the gut draws blood supply there. Also, you will have noticed how blood supply is increased to a part of the body that is warmed. If you put your hand in hot water it goes pink. Drinking hot milk does the same thing for the gut.

Though the brain's blood supply is pretty well protected, the increased blood supply passing to the stomach and intestines causes a slight fall in the supply to the brain. This is part of what causes the drowsiness that helps you go to sleep after your bedtime milky drink. Unlike the sleep-inducing effects of alcohol, this effect keeps going undiminished year after year. Try it and see.

Exercise

The body uses sleep as a way of recuperating after the physical (and mental) rigours of the day. If there haven't been any rigours, sleep is deemed unnecessary. To sleep soundly, it is wise to take some exercise every day. Jumping in and out of the car and raising the glass to your lips don't count. Regular exercise (taken sensibly, according to your level of fitness) is, of course, good for your health anyway, and there is increasing evidence that it helps combat stress and improve your mood.

Of course, this only applies when you are well (even if stressed). Exercise is protective against developing clinical depression, but in the depths of the illness, in any more than very small bursts, makes it worse and delays recovery. So, if you are suffering from depression, hold your horses; wait until you have recovered, then get as fit as you like.

Heat and ventilation

It may seem to be wasteful to have the heating on and the bedroom window open, but this can be very helpful for sleep. Being very hot or cold inhibits sleep, as does a stuffy atmosphere. It is surprising how high the carbon dioxide concentration can get in a room with windows and door closed and two people sleeping in it. This stale air tends to retard falling asleep and cause interruptions in the pattern of sleep through the night.

Meals

Eating at regular times helps to develop a pattern which the body clock can follow. Of course, this isn't always possible if you have a job with irregular hours or are looking after a baby, but the nearer you can get to a regular pattern of eating times, the better your sleep is likely to be. The same applies to other aspects of your life. An uncertain lifestyle without any routine does not encourage the body to develop the rhythms that lead to a regular sleep–wake cycle. It is important, as far as possible, to go to bed at roughly the same time most evenings and to retire neither hungry nor overfull.

Books, TV, etc.

It is unfortunate that the TV companies tend to put on horror films and cops-and-robbers shows late at night, presumably because this stuff is an ideal filler for when most people have gone to bed. Watching such a programme can seriously damage your sleep because, whatever its quality, it is arousing, with lots of death and destruction and the obligatory ploy to make you jump out of your seat just when you thought the hero/heroine was safe. Another annoying thing that I have noticed is that late-night television announcers (and weather forecasters) talk to you as if you were a two-year-old child. This high-pitched smiling patter makes my blood boil. If it does the same to you, I would suggest turning the sound down in between programmes.

The brain is not designed to pass rapidly from a state of arousal to sleep, so anything exciting, annoying or upsetting is likely to delay the onset of sleep. The same is true of books; I would advise against thrillers at bedtime for this reason. Go for something less exciting; a magazine perhaps. For the last two years I have been reading *A la recherche du temps perdu* by Marcel Proust (in English – I'm terrible at languages) at the rate of half a page a night. It is a lovely book, beautifully written, with touches of soft humour, but nothing whatever happens in it and at around 6,000 pages I think that it should last longer than me.

A warning here about bringing work home with you. One insomniac assured me that he had supper at 8.30 every evening and then curled up for a couple of hours to read before retiring at 11 p.m. every night, but still he couldn't sleep. On closer questioning, it emerged that what he was reading was journals on investment in order to maximize his profits as a stockbroker. He admitted to 'getting a real buzz out of it'. Anyone who has studied knows that it takes a great deal of concentration and effort. You need at least a couple of hours relaxing or doing something useless before your brain will be ready to sleep.

Sex

Here is sometimes a major source of discord between couples. After sex, most women become more alert while most men tend to fall asleep. This is due to different effects of sexual intercourse on the nervous system of the two sexes and has become the source of many a gag for comedians, professional and amateur. For insomniac men (and occasionally women) this fact can be a useful point to take into account when considering the evening's agenda. Approach this carefully, though; an invitation such as 'How about it, then, because I want a good sleep' just won't do.

The repository of thoughts

You've had a very busy day; no time to think. I know it well. You get home late, have supper, have a chat and go to bed. At last you have the time and space to review the day and think what is needed for tomorrow. Suddenly you remember some essential task and you are worried that you will forget it by the morning. You work the problem through in your mind and it worries you because this problem throws up a whole load of others. Now you have several things on your mind and you try to sort them out and log them in your brain so that you will remember what you have to do tomorrow. Then you try to go to sleep, but you can't.

It's hardly surprising. How can you expect to sleep when you have programmed your brain to solve problems? The trouble is that if you try to exclude these thoughts from your mind they keep popping back. However hard you try, you can't clear your mind ready for slumber.

The brain is like that. It won't let something rest until it is sorted out or at least pigeon-holed. So pigeon-hole it.

Keep a notepad by your bed. Every time a thought or problem comes into your head, write it down. Also write down a time in the morning when you will work out your plan to sort out each problem. For example, 7.30–8.00 a.m. sort out problems: (1) agenda for meeting; (2) sort out holiday arrangements; (3) phone bank manager about overdraft.

By putting your thoughts on to paper, you take them out of your brain; but it will continue to worry unless you reassure it with a guarantee of a time when all will be made right. So when 7.30 a.m. comes, you must address your problem list, though it may well seem less important in the cold light of day.

Forgiveness

As I have said, many people use bedtime as a time to reflect on the day. You tend to focus on the annoying parts. You remember the incidents when someone was rude or somehow got one over on you. 'If only I had been quicker,' you muse, 'I could have made a stinging reply. That would have really put him in his place.' So you plan out what devastating rejoinder you are going to throw at him tomorrow. All of this gets you quite worked up and, of course, you can't sleep.

This is a complete waste of time because never in the history of human experience has anyone been known to carry through the plan the next day. When the morning comes, it all seems trivial, and to seek the person out just to vent your spleen would be very silly. The fact is that in the darkness and solitude of the night, issues and feelings become magnified and only the next day do they resume realistic proportions.

So, in order to sleep well the rule is that everyone is forgiven everything at night-time. This takes some practice but can be done. The next day, you can lay plans for murder if you wish; that is entirely your affair. But no recriminations at night.

Paradoxical injunction

This is based on the established psychological principle that many people unconsciously tend to resist instructions or orders, whoever they come from. They are not trying to be awkward, the mind just works that way. Sometimes a therapist will help someone to change an entrenched behaviour by giving them the opposite instruction from what is really desired, in order to overcome this resistance.

I have experienced this myself. When studying for exams, I always found the prospect of getting down to a solid session of work made me feel like going to sleep. The more urgently I told myself that I must do it, the sleepier I felt. This was strange because it could happen even in the middle of the morning. As soon as the exam was over I would never feel sleepy in the morning; to try to sleep then would be impossible. My brain was unconsciously resisting my order to work.

This phenomenon can be used to your advantage. Choose your least favourite task (for me it would be ironing) and timetable it for about half an hour after your usual bedtime. The prospect of the task may cause you to be asleep by the appointed time. If not, then time when you would otherwise have been uselessly fretting in bed will be put to good use. The achievement of this chore will tend to make you more relaxed and help you to sleep afterwards.

Using these tips should improve your sleep. But if you are still ill with clinical depression, they won't work until you are quite a bit better. Just hold on; your sleep, like everything else, will improve with time.

11

Depressive illness is a political issue

We should be ashamed of ourselves.

Not those with clinical depression, but the rest of us. Throughout the Western world we have for years just stood and watched as our best citizens keep getting this horrid illness, offering them only blame, contempt and condescension. We Brits have been the world's worst at this.

If we are to protect our best sons and daughters and through them escape our latter-day tendency to mediocrity, we must start realizing that people who develop depressive illness need to be respected and nurtured. They are our doers and shakers; if we fail to recognize this, we will all lose.

For this to happen a radical change will have to happen in our attitudes and the way we allow our institutions to operate. At present our society from the top down is based on conflict and blame. Administrative formalities dominate our working lives, we worship change for change's sake and creativity is abandoned in favour of identifying and punishing mistakes.

Politics, the law and the press

You don't have to be a bad person to be a politician, but it certainly helps. I've met quite a few politicians and know people who have met many others. They are a pretty cynical and self-centred bunch on the whole, though there are exceptions. Given the selection system it's not surprising; would you put yourself up for public office? I wouldn't feel important or qualified enough and neither would any of my friends. The system selects for people with great self-belief, who like arguing. It is thus natural that our political system is adversarial and polarized. The result is that the sensible middle ground, in which honest and diligent people thrive, is lost in a mêlée of discord and recrimination. Change happens by revolution, rather than by considered osmosis. In this frantic environment, the cynics adapt, while the straightforward tryers go under.

Take the health service. I have watched over the last two decades as successive governments have changed its structures this way, then that, then back again, all in the name of progress. In fact, all that has been achieved is that the organization has been wrecked, turned into a 'Department of Administrative Affairs' in which the opportunists who pretend to believe in the latest politically dictated silliness rise to the top, while the foot soldiers collapse under the weight of bureaucracy. If anything goes wrong a scapegoat is found and pilloried, while nobody admits that the real problem has been caused by political interference and the fallacy that 'new is best'. The best people give it their all, despite their misgivings, and inevitably go under, through fear and exhaustion, leaving those who care less about you and more about themselves, to treat you.

The fact that making too many changes causes more problems than it solves is not news, or it shouldn't be. The following quote illustrates this:

> My job brought me to realize that frequent reorganization creates a wonderful illusion of progress, while in fact leading only to widespread demoralization and demotivation.

That was written in AD 66 by Caius Petronius, commander of a Roman legion. You would have thought our politicians would have learnt this lesson by now. But then, if they weren't changing things all the time, we might start asking what purpose they were serving . . .

All public servants are vulnerable to this pernicious trend in our society. The professions that I see most frequently with depressive illness are doctors, nurses, social workers, fire fighters, ambulance crew and police officers; predictably; it's always the best ones who get ill. Then, when the system has used them up, such that they are so damaged that they can't work any more, the government makes it increasingly hard for them to retire on medical grounds. What a cheek! Look, politicians, **it isn't these honest workers that are the problem, it's you**.

But it isn't just politicians; they reflect a wider pattern in our culture also represented in our legal system and the press. We have an adversarial legal system that I see unnecessarily injuring people every day. The most obvious example is divorce. While some progress is being made on this, I still frequently see ordinary, honest people at their most vulnerable having their hurt and anger stoked up by the lawyers, causing pain to both combatants that could so easily have been avoided. Indeed, the system insists upon conflict. At present, two people who can't live together any more are still obliged to apportion blame in order to be allowed to move on with their lives. In the process, many a good person develops a depressive illness.

The increasingly punitive and adversarial nature of our society is grist to the mill of our press and other media. When any newsworthy event occurs, the hunt is on for someone to blame. The press and politicians call this 'accountability'. In fact, it is a base human instinct to lash out when hurt, together, I'm afraid, with an instinct sadistically to relish other people's pain and misfortune. It does terrible harm and paralyses good people. In the summer of 2001, I took a friend to Lord's cricket ground to watch our lot get hammered by the Aussies. Unfortunately, she is Australian. The worst thing was her sympathy; it would have been better had she jeered and told me that our lot couldn't beat the Australian Under 9s XI. Instead, she looked for anything positive she could find in the England team's sorry performance. Eventually she gave up and made an observation that was indisputably true: 'Your boys don't look as if they're trying. Look, that one's not even running in to field the ball; it looks as if he doesn't care.' Indeed, the whole team were slouching around, looking cool and detached, as if playing a dull game on the beach with a group of small children. They were smiling and chatting between overs. You wouldn't believe they were being given one of the most appalling drubbings the game has ever seen.

The reason for their apparent detachment was fear. The English players knew that the opposition was the best cricket team ever to take the field and that they would probably be beaten even if they played out of their skins. They also knew that our press would ignore these facts and would attack each and every one of them with relish after the defeat. How do you prevent your spirit being crushed, given this impossible situation? Simple – stop caring, detach yourself emotionally from the situation. Children do this when in abusive situations, only to find as adults that they can't shake off the strategy when they need to engage emotionally with a loved one.

Our cricketers were using the defence of an abused child, and it wasn't their fault. My antipodean friend pointed out that it isn't that way down under. Six months earlier the Australian team had been unexpectedly beaten in India. Their press, according to her, reacted to this reverse in a balanced way, pointing out that even a very good team can lose and that the defeat was an opportunity to learn from the strengths of their opponents. They did so, to devastating effect. I give a lion's share of the credit to their press.

At the time of writing, England has reversed the trend and started winning. Our press has gone wild with excitement and praise, but is already setting up a pedestal for the victorious players, so that, as soon as they falter, as they surely will – that is the way with sport – the hacks will have a great time knocking them off. Wonderful copy, but no good for the long-term success of our team. To succeed, you must allow failure.

If you punish failure, you ensure failure, as nothing is as stifling as fear. If you see defeat as an opportunity, not to be welcomed but studied calmly and developed, your opportunity has no bounds. So abandon the 'English Defence' against the disappointment of failure (pretending not to care and not really trying). Don't take your values from politicians or the press. Learn from your own experience, being sure to treat yourself benignly while you learn, and don't expect to achieve perfection in an imperfect system. Oh, and the same applies to others. Your criticism won't hurt those who deserve it, but you can crush the creativity of the sensitive tryers of the world without meaning to with your ill-judged barbs.

One other thing. Have you noticed how the press is only interested in disasters? When the stock market falls, whole page headlines scream, 'YOUR PENSION IS WORTHLESS. WE'RE ALL DOOMED!' I don't notice any corresponding headlines when the market rises. They should, to be consistent, shout, 'YOU'RE RICH! CRACK OPEN THE BUBBLY AND PREPARE FOR A LIFE OF LUXURY!' They don't.

In fact, they don't make a squeak, because our press is obsessed with creating fear. Why? Does fear really sell? What are we on? Don't believe the doom-mongers. While our world and our future are far from perfect, it's OK and it'll be OK in the end.

Employers

Most employers are getting better, other than the government and its institutions, which are getting worse. The Americans are ahead of us in this regard. Twenty years ago I was seeing large numbers of employees of the American multinationals, who had been made ill by their employers pushing them beyond their capacity. Not any more. These companies have mostly learnt now that it's your best employees who are most at risk of stress-related illness, including clinical depression. They have learnt to nurture their employees, sometimes even to hold back those who seem to be overdoing it. When a diligent worker gets ill, she isn't, on the whole, pushed into returning too quickly, and when she does return she is usually monitored and supported. The organization takes some responsibility for determining why the illness occurred in the first place and for making the necessary changes in the post.

Slowly graded return-to-work packages are arranged. Ideally, these start at around three half-days a week and gradually increase towards full-time working over six weeks to three months, depending on how the employee is faring when her welfare is checked, which happens regularly.

Thus the organization holds on to its most diligent people and recognizes, by a continuing process of trial and error, the maximum sustainable output it can achieve from its workforce. Money spent and time wasted on staff turnover and induction is minimized. What a contrast to the 'use them up and throw them away' attitude of our national institutions!

Protect your best workers; don't assume they will always carry the load they have done. There is a strong temptation to focus your attention on the weakest points in your organization, on the assumption that the strongest will look after themselves. No they won't; they'll look after the company to their last breath, but they won't look after their own needs until forced to do so by illness. If you want to keep them operating, you'll have to watch over them, counselling against overwork if necessary.

Above all, make them realize their worth. I'm not talking about 'investment in people' or other spurious window dressing, like: 'Our workforce is our greatest asset, we value you all and think you're all great.' Nonsense. Everyone knows you don't mean it. There are some hopeless people in every organization; they can't all be great. No, real caring means thinking about who are the doers and tryers in the firm and giving them real time and caring, especially when they're struggling. This makes cold, hard financial sense, whether you care for them as people or not.

Family and friends

It is a disappointing fact that it is usually those closest to you that treat you the worst when you are down. The reason is that they have come to rely on you. Your strength and reliability have long since become a given. Nobody thanks you for slaving away for them, as you have always done. People tend to organize their perceptions to suit themselves and to rationalize away their guilt. There is often no one more vindictive than someone in your debt, or more punishing than someone who is guilty.

So, while your friend or your spouse realizes in his heart of hearts that he has contributed to you becoming ill, through his excessive demands and insufficient support, he will tend to deny and minimize your illness and to blame you for letting him down. Of course, for many I'm exaggerating a bit here, but most of us find it difficult to come to terms with the fact that things have to change and that we can't rely on our rock in the way we always have done. We tend to stamp our feet and sulk a bit.

But look, if you are in the company of someone who has this illness, your friend/spouse is still the same solid, caring person she always was. It will just mean shifting the balance a bit. Protect your asset. You have the privilege of being with one of the world's givers. Thank your lucky stars and give a bit back. No, I don't mean go and earn more money so you can take your partner on an exotic holiday or buy him/her a flashy present. I mean, sit down with your loved one and work out how she can feel more valued while doing a bit less.

To the recently recovered sufferer from clinical depression, I say this: don't waste time blaming your spouse/friends for neglecting your needs or for their lack of gratitude for all that you've done. Take responsibility for your own life, health and happiness. Nobody forced you to do what you do. Those around you put upon you *because you let them*. Now make another choice and take time and space for yourself. Don't expect them to be happy about it; they'll take time to adjust, but adjust they will. And what's more, you'll find they give you more, too. The guilt and loss of self-esteem that results from giving up the role of 'she who will always provide' is temporary. The better balance in your life and the rewards this brings will be permanent.

Some partners remain supportive throughout the illness and the recovery process. These are great people, as it is pretty awful living through an episode of clinical depression in your nearest and dearest. Don't forget to acknowledge this when you get well. This has been a nightmare for you both, though it has been the fault of neither of you.

12

What's the point?

Having struggled through Chapter 11, you could be forgiven for thinking that I have a pretty bleak view of my country, and indeed life itself. But I haven't. I like England (from April to September) and I'm quite fond of life really, though there are times when I'd sell it for a bag of marbles. I've just identified those aspects of my environment that distress and anger me. I'll try to change what I can, this book being one such attempt, but the rest I'll accept, experiencing what today brings.

I believe that one of the main secrets to getting the most out of life is to know what angers you. Express it, do what you can about it, then avoid the people and institutions that are responsible for generating it as much as you can. If you don't like where you are, then make another choice. Yes, I know I get a bit boring, banging on about choices, but identifying them, making them and then accepting the consequences of them will allow you to control your life. If you can make them based on what you really want and be generous to yourself when you get them wrong, you've got a great chance of staying healthy, and maybe even achieving contentment.

I didn't like the system in which I worked in the NHS. I tried to change it at a local level, but then when I found that the politicians had already colonized it and divided it up among themselves, my blood pressure started rising, so I left. I used to do a lot of legal work, but then the dishonesty and shoddiness of the system started to get to me, so I turned away. I'm still working with the press, because some of them are OK and I think I can use them to help get my messages across, but if it starts to make me, in the eyes of my friends, a bitter person, I will stop.

Most people are really quite good, most of the time. If that isn't your experience, you are letting the users of the world take too much of your life. They'll do that for as long as you let them, because they have a keen sense of who they can use and how much.

The givers and doers, like you, will tend to collect these types. I would suggest you try to identify them and get them out of your life. Or if you are married to one, decide on your limits and boundaries, and stick to them.

The same applies to work. Most employers aren't abusive, but maybe you work for one that is. They select your type, and as other, less diligent employees leave quite quickly, you'll tend to find yourself increasingly alone in your plight. Unless, that is, you decide to take charge, stop being abused and change the way you operate, or if that is impossible, leave. You assume that no other employer will have you, but in fact you are an employer's dream. If you don't make a move, nothing will change; if you do, you are opting for a bit of risk and a lot of opportunity.

You see, life can be better. Not that you can, or should, suddenly divest yourself of all your responsibilities. But if you decide that you are going to be responsible for yourself and your happiness, rather than being responsible for other people and theirs and then resenting the fact that nobody does the same for you, you'll be surprised how things can change. And then if you stop demanding that everyone approves of you all the time, or that life gives you what you seek instantly – now, that's exciting. Yes, this is true, even if you have three small children to look after, or are president of the World Bank.

You may feel that this way of thinking is selfish, or un-Christian. I don't think it is. Is it better to give away your last seedlings to your hungry brothers to eat now, or to plant them, so that they, you and many others may thrive in the future? I suggest that even you don't know how much good you'll be able to do if you stay well.

My patients have taught me so much. What a privilege it has been to have learned from the experiences and suffering of so many good people. They have even given me some sense of what life is for. If my reading of their lives is right, it's for making choices and learning from their results, for finding positives in whichever situation befalls you, for finding a balance, for love, for fun and for forgiveness, particularly of yourself.

You and I have made plenty of mistakes, but please don't condemn yourself for not having had hindsight when you made yours. The episode from which you, or someone close to you, have, hopefully, emerged was an opportunity, terrible though it was. You have confronted the fact that, in your headlong pursuit of excellence or your life's work of trying to please everyone, you missed the point. In fact, though, you have learnt what you never could have done had you or those around you remained well. Come on, you know it's true. You wouldn't have stopped and re-evaluated your life had you not been stopped dead in your tracks. A certain Roman on the road to Damascus comes to mind. Now that it has happened, just make sure you change; if you do, I've got good news for you. You've found the key to a happier life.

The world has goodness, kindness and fun mixed in with the badness, cruelty and oppression. Your task is to sort out the one from the other, while accepting your body's design limits. If you don't overload the fuse, it won't blow; if you do, it will. It's your choice.

In any case you can't achieve that much, whatever you do. Mother Teresa of Calcutta got it right: 'We cannot achieve great things on this earth, we can only do small things with great love.' Pace yourself while you do them. It was a famous golfer (Fred Couples, I think? If not, it should have been, he's so cool!) who urged that, however important the round (and some of his were for fortunes), always find time to stop and smell the flowers. Or in the words of two of my wisest patients, 'However busy, stressed and late you are, don't walk up escalators.'

Hey! I've had enough of this. I think we've done enough in the last hundred-odd pages to deserve a break from thinking about life, for today. You know what to do to change things around. Now, if you want to, do so. If not, oh well. It's your life. And in the words of a dear man who taught and comforted me when I was very small and very alone: 'Life's too short to worry!'

And anyway, tomorrow's Monday. Oh, no!

Useful addresses

British Association for Behavioural and Cognitive Psychotherapies
Imperial House
Hornby Street
Bury
BL9 5BN
Tel.: 0161 705 4304
Website: www.babcp.com
Email: babcp@babcp.com

British Association for Counselling and Psychotherapy
BACP House
15 St John's Business Park
Lutterworth
Leicestershire
LE17 4HB
Tel.: 01455 883300 (8.45 a.m. to 5 p.m.)
Website: www.bacp.co.uk
Email: bacp@bacp.co.uk

Cruse Bereavement Care
PO Box 800
Richmond
Surrey
TW9 1RG
Tel.: 020 8939 9530 (Office)
Daytime Helpline 0844 477 9400
Young persons' freephone helpline 0808 808 1677
Website: www. crusebereavementcare.org.uk
Email: info@cruse.org.uk

Depression Alliance
20 Great Dover Street
London SE1 4LX
Tel.: 0845 123 23 20
Website: www.depressionalliance.org
Email: information@ depressionalliance.org

Mind
15–19 Broadway
London E15 4BQ
Tel.: 020 8519 2122 (Office)
Mind infoline: 0300 123 3393
Website: www.mind.org.uk
Email: contact@mind.org.uk

Priory Group (formerly Priory Healthcare)
21 Exhibition House
Addison Bridge Place
London W14 8XP
Tel.: 01325 331 266
Advice line: 0845 277 4679
Website: www.priorygroup.com
Email: info@priorygroup.com

Samaritans
Helpline: 08457 90 90 90 (24 hours, every day)
(Or write to: Chris, PO Box 9090, Stirling FK8 2SA)
Website: www.samaritans.org
Email: jo@samaritans.org

SANE
First Floor, Cityside House
40 Adler Street
London E1 1EE
Tel.: 020 7375 1002 (Office)
SANEline 0845 767 8000
Website: www.sane.org.uk
Email: info@sane.org.uk

YoungMinds (for children's mental health)
Suite 11, Baden Place
Crosby Row, London SE1 1YW
Tel.: 020 7089 5050
Parents' Helpline: 0808 802 5544
Website: www.youngminds.org.uk
Email: ymenquiries@youngminds. org.uk

Suggested reading

Burns, Dr D., *The Feeling Good Handbook*. London, Plume, 1999.

Burns, Dr D., *10 Days to Great Self-Esteem*. London, Vermilion, 2000.

Dryden, Dr W., *How to Make Yourself Miserable*. London, Sheldon Press, 2001.

Dryden, Dr W., *Overcoming Guilt*. London, Sheldon Press, 1994.

Dryden, Dr W. and Gordon, J., *Think Your Way to Happiness*. London, Sheldon Press, 1990.

Greenberger, D. and Padesky, C., *Mind Over Mood*. New York, Guilford Press, 1995.

Harris, Thomas A., *I'm OK, You're OK*. London, Arrow, 1995.

Kabat-Zinn, J. et al., *The Mindful Way through Depression: Freeing yourself from chronic unhappiness*. New York, Guilford Press, 2007.

Klein, D. and Wender, P., *Understanding Depression*. Oxford, Oxford University Press, 2005.

Norwood, R., *Daily Meditations for Women Who Love Too Much*. London, Arrow, 1986.

Powell, Dr T., *Stressfree Living*. London, Dorling Kindersley, 2001.

Tolle, E., *The Power of Now*. London, Hodder, 2001.

Yapko, M., *Breaking the Patterns of Depression*. London, Doubleday, 1998.

Index